From the files of *THE NATIONAL ENQUIRER*

ROSIE O!

How She Conned America

by Jim Nelson
with Susan Trew

Edited by Nicholas Maier

American Media Inc.

From the files of the National Enquirer:
ROSiE O!
How She Conned America

Copyright © 2003 AMI Books, Inc.

Cover design: Tony Ballester
Interior design: Debbie Duckworth

ISBN: 1-885840-06-3

First printing: April 2003

Printed in the United States of America

10 9 8 7 6 5 4 3 2 1

PROLOGUE

Wʜᴀᴛ ʜᴀᴘᴘᴇɴᴇᴅ ᴛᴏ Rᴏsɪᴇ O'Dᴏɴɴᴇʟʟ?

In one of the most amazing transformations of a celebrity the public has ever witnessed, she's changed basically overnight from the Queen of Nice into a foul-mouthed, proud-to-be-queer political activist.

The gazillion fans of her talk show — and definitely the publishers of "Rosie" magazine — are stunned.

The easy explanation for her sudden metamorphosis is that Rosie finally decided to become in public the same person she has always been in private. In reality, she was never the Queen of Nice, a title that typecast her and eventually suffocated her professionally. Roseann O'Donnell, who said recently she thinks of herself as "Ro," was given the name "Rosie" in her teen years by the emcee of a comedy skit, and she never thought it fit her. The real Rosie is a blunt, quick-tempered, lightning-witted, tough-talking lesbian.

But the moniker helped her talk show become a mega-success, eventually bringing Rosie, or whatever the star calls herself, a $20-million-a-year salary and millions more in endorsements.

Rosie O'Donnell's huge wit, her versatile performing talents and her public image as a down-to-earth mom, brought her phenomenal fame in almost any medium she cared to work in. Rosie was the rare performer who found success in TV, movies, theater, stand-up comedy and publishing.

But she grew to despise the lie that was her public persona. And in 2002, Rosie killed the Queen of Nice, dragged the body through the streets and burned the corpse.

Fans who watched "The Rosie O'Donnell Show" regularly had a pretty good idea that Rosie was a lesbian long before she announced it publicly. Besides the masculine affectations, she had dropped plenty of hints about her sexuality. And although she had never confirmed she was a lesbian, she had never denied it, either.

The fact that she was gay came as no surprise — but the complete transformation of the woman has been absolutely shocking.

In short order, she got a butch haircut and announced that her female partner was pregnant with their baby. And, if there was any doubt that the Queen of Nice was dead, Rosie did a stand-up routine in which she went on an obscenity-laced tirade against other celebrities.

In one of the most reported quotes of 2002, Rosie accurately observed, "The bitch ain't so nice anymore."

The Queen is dead! Long live the Queer!

Rosie also became even more politically active, using her money and fame to try to repeal laws in states that ban gays from adopting children.

To add to the turmoil, Rosie quit her magazine in a nasty dispute with her publisher. She wanted to use the magazine as a platform for her controversial social ideas, claimed the publisher. Rosie said that since the magazine was named after her, she should be able to dictate what it printed. The resulting lawsuits threaten to drain all of the more than $100 million fortune she has amassed as the Queen of Nice.

To say that Rosie finally came out of the closet because she was sick of living a lie is simplistic and not entirely true.

The roots of Rosie's startling recasting of herself are buried much deeper. They lie in the darkly dysfunctional household in which she claims she and her four siblings were raised by her hard-drinking father, Edward O'Donnell. When Rosie was 10, her mother died of breast cancer. The rest of her life has been defined by that event.

"Rosie began being the Queen of Nice when her mother was dying and she had to pretend that everything was fine in order not to upset her mother — and because Rosie had no one to listen to her feelings and comfort her," Beverly Hills psychiatrist Dr. Carole Lieberman told the Enquirer.

"Though she was dubbed The Queen of Nice when she hosted her TV show, Rosie resented it then, too. She's always wanted people to love her for who she was, instead of her having to be 'nice' to get them to love her. This is why she finally gave up her show and revealed to the world what she was really like by coming out of the closet.

"Her resentment, which she'd been hiding for most of her life, finally caused her to rebel."

The National Enquirer has covered Rosie's life in more detail than any other publication. The newspaper was the first to reveal her lesbian romances, reporting her love for women without prejudice — the same way it reported celebrity heterosexual relationships.

And the Enquirer was the first to track down Edward O'Donnell after decades of estrangement and disparagement from his famous daughter.

Although Rosie certainly does not like all that the Enquirer has printed about her, she has granted the paper exclusive interviews about important events in her life. Inside the Enquirer's secret files on Rosie O'Donnell are interviews not only with the star herself, but with hundreds of people who know her intimately and had contact with her as a child, when she suffered the traumas that eventually led to her dizzying transformation in 2002.

Many of the people closest to Rosie spoke to the Enquirer on the condition that their names not be published, so as to preserve their relationship with the star.

In this book — which gives information that has never before been published — these people will tell you about the Rosie the public never sees. They will tell you about the incredible dramas she's experienced when the cameras are not rolling.

They will tell you what really happened to Rosie.

CHAPTER 1

"**I** DON'T REALLY FEEL LIKE A ROSIE," DECLARED THE SIX-TIME EMMY-WINNING DIVA OF DAYTIME TALK SHOWS, RIGHT AFTER SHE CHOSE TO END "THE ROSIE O'DONNELL SHOW" IN 2002.

But what about the obscene amount of money it brought her?

She already had more money than she could ever spend, Rosie O'Donnell told the world.

Just about nobody else in entertainment has ever said that before. You could list them on the wrapper of one of those Ring Dings Ms. O'Donnell was always chowing on camera.

She didn't have the name Rosie until, as a teenager, she delivered in a high school skit a dead-on mimicry of Gilda Radner's character Roseann Rosannadanna, which when filtered through a microphone sounded so much like "Roseann O'Donnell" that the emcee called her Rosie to avoid the confusion.

Why doesn't she see herself as Rosie?

"Rosie is an elderly aunt who forces you to eat

decade-old hard candies that live in the bottom of her crusty purse," she explains. "Rosie never fit me. I feel like a Ro."

And that's what her friends call her.

✳✳✳✳✳

Her life began on March 21, 1962, when she was born in the city-suburb of Commack on Long Island. With a population of about 25,000, less than an hour from New York, Commack was not a rich town, not a poor one. It was in the middle — like Roseann O'Donnell — the third child among five in a working-class family with strong Irish roots. Her father was an engineer-technician named Edward O'Donnell.

There was another Roseann O'Donnell already in the family, the romantic, life-loving woman who was Rosie's mother and total inspiration. Happy and witty and positive, the senior Roseann loved to sing the songs of Hollywood and Broadway, and the numbers of exuberant female vocalists of the day, pop icons whose music Rosie still cherishes, filled the air of the O'Donnell home. Mother, Rosie, and the other kids were always singing along to the records of Barbra Streisand and Bette Midler in the not very grand home on Rhonda Lane.

Their neighborhood wasn't in the upscale part of town, but the O'Donnells weren't poor, either.

"It was that place in-between where it can be difficult to make ends meet and you buy generic-brand everything," adult Rosie recalled in her candid and heartfelt memoir, "Find Me," published in 2002.

The suburban residence where Rosie lived until she was 18 wasn't a bit like the multimillion-dollar homes she would later own. As much the romantic dreamer as her mother, she still couldn't imagine that she would have an estate in Connecticut, two mansions overlooking the Hudson River north of the Big Apple, a grand townhouse in the most expensive part of midtown Manhattan and a luxurious compound with a dock on Star Island near Miami.

The O'Donnell house on Rhonda Lane was "always a mess," Rosie remembers, with no criticism of her mom's efforts to cope with five lively kids. "Laundry in piles, toys with missing pieces and never enough Scotch tape. We had wallpaper with bubbles in it and Magic Marker marked stairs." They drove around Commack in a rusty old blue station wagon.

There was an eighth resident in the house, too. Rosie's spunky maternal grandmother lived in a room on the top floor. Colorful, Irish-American and going deaf, she smoked too many Chesterfields and blasted the sound on her TV. Still in possession of all her marbles and plenty of energy, the spirited old woman delighted the young O'Donnells.

Rosie's father wasn't nearly as upbeat as grandma or anyone else in the house. He worked hard to support the family, but found it wasn't easy for him to get close to his children. He tried, but showing affection wasn't what he did best. As a father he was earnest and reserved.

There was a place, however, where he could avoid facing this difficult situation.

Rosie and one of her brothers have ruefully hinted

that their father sometimes stopped on the way home for a drink or two in a local bar, where he could unwind. The children wanted those hours with their father, they recall, but it wasn't something the family discussed.

If her husband was something of a private person, the senior Roseann was exuberantly social. She enjoyed people, and plenty of people enjoyed her. Even the teachers at Rolling Hills Elementary School found Rosie's mother cheerily funny and charming. When they spotted her round face and full figure in the hallway, they'd come grinning from classrooms because they knew this warm and witty woman would make them laugh.

She was all earthy and without pretension.

A delightful natural entertainer.

Sound familiar?

"I remember that she was funny," Rosie said of her mother. "I remember her coming to my elementary school and all the teachers would go out of the room to talk to her. They'd say to us, 'Read your books. We'll be right back.' There were glass windows along the hallway, and I remember my mom making all the teachers laugh. Once, I went to a PTA meeting with her, and she went up to speak and had everyone laughing. I remember feeling like that was an amazing thing, and wanting to be like her in that way."

Rosie's mother set a big example for her in ways beyond comedy. Her mother is a big reason that Rosie has become so renowned for her positive attitude and many community services.

"My mom was an active lady, president of our school PTA, a member of the parish council and a

Girl Scout troop leader," her dynamic daughter recalls proudly.

As a child, she thought her mother was absolutely wonderful.

She still thinks so.

This deep love for her mother, solid and big as a mountain, is a key to who Rosie O'Donnell is, what she does, and ultimately, who she will be. And it was the loss of her mother that was to color everything that came after, to this day.

❋❋❋❋❋

"Your mother has passed away."

With only these words, Edward O'Donnell informed his young children, gathered in the kitchen, that their vivacious beloved mother had died. The children weren't completely sure what the tactful phrase actually meant. They thought they knew, but it was vague.

In the O'Donnell house, as in most houses, there were truths told and there were lies, and there were some things that were never, ever spoken. Rosie learned this when she was around 10 years old and observed that her mother was ill and wasn't getting better.

Her parents didn't tell her how serious the situation was. At first, they tried to avoid the subject so they wouldn't frighten the children. Later, when it became clear that something had to be said, a tense and troubled Edward O'Donnell pretended that the problem was hepatitis.

Then a fifth-grade student, Rosie had been

frequently encouraged by her mother to look words up in the large household dictionary. Now she dutifully scanned its worn pages for information about "hepatitis" and learned that it might be transmitted by dirty needles. Practical young Rosie somberly vowed never to use a sewing machine.

At this difficult time, she recognized that the medical concern that kept her parents from giving her much attention wasn't improving. She couldn't let loneliness defeat her. She understood that she had to take care of herself now.

And she did so in some remarkable ways — in Rosie ways — ways that foreshadowed her future stardom as a creative improvisational entertainer. She taught herself card tricks, how to juggle, how to balance a chair in the palm of her hand, how to spin a ball on a finger, and feats in a variety of sports — softball, basketball, tennis and others.

Rosie saw her mother's health fade steadily. Even as her mom made trips to the hospital, Rosie wasn't told that she was battling breast cancer. To add to the grim tension, the hospital had an old-fashioned rule against child visitors, so Edward O'Donnell had to smuggle in his worried daughter.

Fittingly, perhaps, this vibrant Irish-American woman died on Saint Patrick's Day in 1973, a week before Rosie's 11th birthday.

Rosie was visiting her best friend, who lived nearby. The two girls were playing Mystery Date with no idea the whole world was about to change.

A phone call led her friend's mother, a woman who is still close to Rosie, to tell her she needed to go home. Soon the five O'Donnell children were waiting uneasily in their kitchen while their father spoke softly with other adults in the dining room. He entered the kitchen to say those five words to his children:

"Your mother has passed away."

Rosie didn't cry at first. She went outside to play hockey, pondering what her father said.

"I think I went numb," Rosie recalled years later. "It was the kind of grief that leaves a wound that's hard to heal. I don't know if it ever fully heals."

She didn't cry at her mother's funeral, either.

She couldn't, because she wasn't taken to the funeral, and neither was her sister. Nobody told them why they weren't allowed to go to the funeral, but back then families would sometimes "spare" young girls that possibly traumatic experience. Subsequently, the two sisters were driven in the family's old blue station wagon to the obligatory traditional wake, where everyone cried. As the adults released their grief, Rosie and her sister stood by scared and sobbing, not knowing what to do.

They were defenseless . . . devastated.

It was a landmark — the landmark — that would change Rosie's life.

Saint Patrick's Day and Mother's Day remain deeply painful times in the life of Rosie O'Donnell. Her bond with her mother is as overwhelming as ever.

So is Rosie's dread of the illness that took her mother's life. Since childhood, she's lived with an intense fear of breast cancer. Much less was known about it when her mother succumbed, and lack of knowledge was a dangerous situation for women who urgently needed and deserved much better information, diagnosis and treatment. It was something that many people wouldn't talk about back then. Since becoming a gigantic star, Rosie has used her fame to publicize the need for open discussion of breast cancer and the need for early, potentially lifesaving treatment.

"My whole life revolves around my mother's death," Rosie has told friends. "It changed who I was as a person. I don't know who I would be if my mother lived — but I would trade it all to see."

CHAPTER 2

THE REALITY OF HER MOTHER'S DEATH WAS TERRIBLY HARD FOR 11-YEAR-OLD ROSIE O'DONNELL TO ACCEPT. SHE COPED BY DOING WHAT MANY CHILDREN AND ADULTS DO IN SUCH BITTER SITUATIONS. SHE TRIED TO AVOID REALITY.

For many months Rosie took refuge in a fantasy that her beloved mother wasn't actually dead at all. Her mom had chosen to seek a less difficult and happier life elsewhere, the little girl told herself.

California, of course.

California, land of so many people's dreams and the golden place to children of all ages, including the hopeful legions who yearned for movie or television stardom. Young Rosie tried to believe that her mother had held her breath in the coffin, played dead, and then escaped to enjoy a carefree life as a hippie flower vendor in California, free of the burden of raising five children.

Young Rosie developed other cover stories to help her cope with her mother's death. "Patty Hearst had just been kidnapped, so I came up with a fantasy that

that was what had happened to my mom too, and nobody was telling us," she said.

And she used plain old-fashioned denial to cope — even into her college days. "People would call and ask, 'Is your mother home?'" she said. "And I would say, 'She's in the shower, can you call back?' And one day my college roommate asked, 'Why do you always talk about your father, and never your mother?' I stopped for a moment, and I remember having to choke the words out: 'Well, she died.' That was the first time I ever said it. When my mom died, I just shut down emotionally. You're angry, you're wounded. You use coping mechanism after coping mechanism."

Just as many children wonder whether they are to blame for their parents' divorce, Rosie also took responsibility for her mother's departure.

As the fantasy slowly faded, the difficulty of living with their sad and distant father set in. It was soon clear that he couldn't give his children what their mother had cheerfully provided every day.

Rosie's father was also coping in his own way with his grief over his wife's passing, and rid the house of photos and other memorabilia of the senior Roseann O'Donnell.

Asked once if she looked like her mom, Rosie said: "Yes, although we don't have many photos. My father didn't keep a lot of stuff. In his effort to get over his own grief, he made some rash decisions about photos and things like that."

School didn't help Rosie deal with her loss. In fact, it unintentionally intensified her pain. Her mother had been the very giving and popular head of the Parents Teacher Association, and her fellow PTA members, wanting to honor her, got permission from the school to put up a plaque in her memory.

They couldn't guess how the bereft Rosie would react to this gesture of affection. Every time Rosie walked past it, she ached. It reminded her again and again of her irreplaceable mother, and her pain began to build until she lost control.

She had to escape.

She ran away from home and didn't show up at school. Dozens of people went looking for her. The one who found her and persuaded her to come back was her older brother, Danny. Of course, it wasn't a really nourishing home that met her needs. "No one ever said 'I love you' in our house" after her mother died, she remembers. Seeking love and comfort, Rosie began to spend more and more time at the nearby residence of her best friend, Jackie Ellard, whose mother, Bernice, was kind and caring to her.

"Bernice took me in as one of her own," Rosie recalled. "She was the first adult to say, 'I love you,' and give me a big hug after my mom died. She became a mother figure to me. She was a divorced parent with two daughters of her own, but she always made me feel I had a place."

"When we'd go to the mall together, people would say, 'Your daughters look so much alike!'" Rosie said. "Bernice would answer: 'Guess which one isn't mine?' and they'd always guess wrong."

Rosie reciprocates their affection to this day. She recalls warmly how good and satisfying life was in their house where a woman's touch was so visible, so right. They welcomed her to dinner three or four times a week.

Rosie liked everything about the warm Ellard household, including the kid-friendly junk food. "Mrs. Ellard had everything," she recalled years later. "Dixie Riddle Cups and single-sized bags of Fritos, Cool Whip and serving spoons. They had serving dishes. And gravy, not just at Thanksgiving. And real Tupperware with lids that matched and 'the burps' instead of margarine containers."

"Every year I send a Christmas card to Bernice and I tell her all the Ellard things I have in my house," Rosie said in 1996. "I have an electric knife that cuts the meat thin. And Tupperware with the right kinds of lids. I have Ziploc bags instead of the folded sandwich bags. These were all things that the Ellards had that I always wanted.

"In our house, we always ran out. Our socks didn't match and our underwear didn't fit — just those little motherly touches that were really missing. I wanted a home like the Ellards."

The Ellard daughters had clean hair with perfect parts that Rosie envied. Her own locks were so full of tangles that once the school nurse had to cut the knots out. When Rosie told her father that the Ellards had a spray called No More Tangles for their girls, he ignored her request that he buy it.

"He had a dead wife and five small kids," the star reflected recently. "No More Tangles was not a priority."

All these things Rosie wanted were small from an adult's point of view, but they certainly were not to a lonely, motherless child who felt deprived and afraid. She hungered for all the reassuring symbols of a "regular" suburban life with two parents and the comfort foods advertised pervasively in our culture.

"I'd come home from school and the house wasn't clean like the neighbors' because there was no mom there to do it," she recalled.

Even before she hit her teens, Rosie had a whopping appetite for junk food, and she soon succumbed to a food addiction. With sugar and spice, literally, she subconsciously built around her a fortress protecting her from a sharp sense of isolation and loss. Today, after many years of psychotherapy, it is almost certain that this intelligent woman knows she's been filling herself up because she's felt desperately empty.

There's another reason she overeats, she's told friends: In the back of her mind she dreads ending up gaunt as her mother was in the final months. Even as Rosie started to put on the pounds in her teen years, she couldn't shake the mental image of her "thick-waisted Irish mother" wasting away as the cancer devastated her.

"My mother got very thin before she died," Rosie confided in a candid interview. "I was a child and I didn't really understand this. But I associated getting thin with getting sick and going away.

"As I grew up emotionally, all of the issues surrounding weight that deal with emotions came to the forefront for me," she said in the interview. "As I became a grown-up, I had to deal with these issues, and with them came weight, because the way people deal with problems is often with food, which is a symptom of another thing."

And what goes with junk food in a teenager's life?

Especially one looking for escape in her motherless house?

TV, of course.

"Leave It to Beaver," "Eight Is Enough" and "The Brady Bunch" were favorite staples of the O'Donnell kids.

Was it a coincidence that they all had a healthy, cheery and supportive mother starring in them?

"My whole family became fixated on TV," Rosie recalled. "I think it was some sort of surrogate parenting. I wanted Eight Is Enough to happen to my family, you know? I wanted Abby — or some widow — to come and be my mom. I lived all my emotional life through movies or TV. I would see a movie and cry and cry, but not about my own loss or pain — about what was happening in the movie. That's the way it is to this day."

Those sappy, now-classic shows of the 1970s "offered a way we could feel all the things in our family we couldn't say," Rosie said. "The Partridge Family and The Brady Bunch became surrogate families for me. Little House on the Prairie, Room 222 — those shows allowed me to access my emotions."

And the musical heritage their late mother left in her small selective record collection survived to help. Rosie memorized performances by Barbra Streisand and Bette Midler, still icons to her today.

Rosie never did things by half. Smitten with handsome teen star David Cassidy, she gazed up at a poster of him on her drab bedroom wall and daydreamed about him and his glamorous world. Although most of her girlfriends at Commack

South High School were also in their bedrooms romanticizing like this about young TV stars, Edward O'Donnell's middle child did more than that. She made up her mind that she would be a television star too.

Someday. Somehow. She'd do whatever it took.

Such determination is not uncommon among middle children. Psychologists have studied it, and many mothers and fathers who never took a psychology course have seen it first-hand. Not all middle children have this extraordinary resolve, but so many do that it's widely recognized. It can help them do very well in life. It's a way to be noticed, and that's good for the self-esteem of anyone at any age.

Television promised a better life for Rosie than the one in the sad house on Rhonda Lane. Her father wasn't getting any better at coping with his wife's death and the emotional and practical demands of caring for five children. People who've known the O'Donnells for years remember that the children tried not to complain about nights when their unhappy dad came home late after drinking, and his only communication with his five frightened kids was to shout in frustration.

The oldest child, Danny, who was three years Rosie's senior, tried to help his brothers and sisters. Caring for others seemed to come naturally to him. Soft-spoken and the most studious of the quintet, he eventually became an attorney and a political idealist who has fought for tenants and others who need protection from the powerful. Long active in the Democratic Party on Manhattan's liberal Upper West Side, he was elected to the New York State Assembly in November 2002.

Following in his footsteps at Commack South High School, Rosie did fairly well in her courses when she began to heal somewhat after her mother's death. But there were plenty of bumps through adolescence as Rosie struggled with her mom's absence.

Bernice Ellard took her to buy her first bra and tried to fill the void left by her mom's death in other ways, but Rosie continued to miss her mother. "It was traumatic when a girl gets her period and her mom is not there to comfort her," she said. "It's incredibly painful."

She wasn't quite as good a student as her brother, but what she did excel at was a sign of things to come. Her singing and acting talents and flair for comedy won her parts in drama society plays and musicals, including the Senior Follies. She whacked the drums in a high school rock band, won a place as a cheerleader, and made the varsity tennis squad.

"I was on every sports team," she's recalled. "I played softball and volleyball and tennis and basketball. A regular tomboy jock girl and proud of it."

Rosie impressed her classmates with her exuberance, hilarious humor and willingness to work on an awesome assortment of projects. She was building herself a reputation as a doer. The middle child didn't want to be taken for granted.

What this hopeful, helpful, driven teenager did want was to be liked and needed. And, in fact, she was becoming liked and needed by more and more of her Commack classmates, which gave her confidence a shot in the arm. By the time she was 16, she had the self-assurance to tell her friends that she was definitely, absolutely going to be a star.

Ironically, Rosie now credits the void her mother's death left in the home, and her father's emotional distance, with giving her the wherewithal to be a leader.

"Because there was a lack of guidance in the house, I looked inside myself," she said once. "Some kids fall apart in that situation and others become their own leader. I became my own leader and made rules for myself."

"Rosie had to be her own parent," recalled high school friend Jeanne Davis. "She threw herself into everything and became a take-charge person. We used to butt heads all the time, because she would try to order dinner for me and then she'd want to pay the bill."

She was clearly serious about being a star — and her mother's premature death only imparted a sense of urgency in young Rosie. "I remember thinking at ten years old, if I was going to die in my thirties, what would I want to have achieved?" she recalled. "It made me strive for my goals with a fervent passion."

She said that besides the gift of easy laughter her mother bestowed upon her, her family used comedy to deal with things. "After our mother died, if you wanted to express something painful, you could only do it couched in comedy," she said.

Rosie learned to use comedy to obtain the approval of grown-ups — to her ever-lasting benefit. Acting in a high school revue, she one night brought down the house delivering a perfect imitation of Gilda Radner's Roseann Rosannadanna. "I didn't care about the kids," she said. "I wanted to make the adults laugh."

She did that. In fact, she did such a great job that a parent in the audience suggested that she audition at his comedy club. Since she'd already performed at the open-mike night of the local Ground Round restaurant, she decided to give it a try. After watching Jerry Seinfeld on the "Merv Griffin Show," she went to the club the following night and performed his act.

She remembers it as if it were yesterday.

"I killed," she recalled. "Everybody was screaming, 'That girl is so funny!' Then I walked off the stage and all the comics descended upon me: 'You can't do that! Where'd you get those jokes?'

"'Well, forget it,'" Rosie says she told the comics. "'I'm not doing this. When you're an actress, they don't ask you to write the movie.' I was so mad. I was sixteen and I thought they were ridiculous."

Rosie faced the fact that she wasn't ready to create a comedy routine of her own, so she decided she couldn't perform before paying adults until she knew a lot more. A young and underage Ms. O'Donnell managed to talk her way or sneak into a number of comedy clubs to advance her showbiz education and learn by watching the professionals honing their acts there. And her eyes turned to the razzle-dazzle of Broadway's booming musical theater.

How could she get in to see those fabulous shows?

Rosie's smarts, imagination and willingness to work were her answer then, just as they are today. The high school junior earned money in part-time jobs during afternoons and, it's said, "borrowed" small amounts of money from her father's pocket.

Her limited funds in hand, she'd cut classes once in a while on a Wednesday afternoon to rush into Manhattan to see part of a Broadway musical. She didn't have enough to cover the cost of a matinee ticket, but since she was cute and clearly a fan, sympathetic ushers would grin and let the kid sneak in for the second act.

Rosie O'Donnell is still grateful for that help. Her vivid memory of her Wednesday afternoons as a high school kid at the theaters are one reason for her extraordinary commitment to help, in many ways and at immense expense, other children — and Broadway — today.

She also made sure to earn decent grades at Commack South High School. At the same time, she was the hub of her class's extracurricular activities. She may not have been fully recognized in the house on Rhonda Lane, but at Commack South everyone knew Rosie O'Donnell.

In 1980, the tomboy jock girl was voted senior class president, class clown and homecoming queen. Her friends deemed her the "most spirited" in the entire school. She took her duties seriously. When the senior prom neared, she wasn't shy about asking one of the handsomest boys in her class to be her date.

"She told me that she had a boyfriend and she knew I had a girlfriend," recalled that boy, now a married fireman. "She thought that she and I would make a powerhouse couple for this special night. She was right. It was a friendly thing — social not physical. We both had a swell time."

Old pal Jeanne Davis remembered Rosie as always

following the beat of a different drum in high school.

"She was different from the rest of us in so many ways," Davis recalled. "We'd all go out, and while we'd be drinking with false ID's, she'd be playing video games. Rosie was so isolated. Yet she managed to always be the most popular."

As her high school years ended, Rosie did not have a great desire to go on to college, but she wanted to follow in Danny's footsteps. And she knew that her mother, who had always steered her to the dictionary when she was a little girl, would have been proud of her if she tried.

Although she later made him a punching bag in her comedy routines, her father worked hard to support his five children. But times were tighter for the O'Donnells than for other teens in Commack, Rosie recalled.

"We weren't poor," Rosie said. "My father was an electrical engineer. But there were five children. The kids who went to school with us would all get Camaros on their sixteenth birthdays. And at our house, we had a Plymouth Volare with an AM radio. All five of us kids had to use that car. We went to the flea market to buy clothes, not Macy's."

Still, with her father's earnings and her own good grades, there was enough money to send the children to college — if they wanted to go. Rosie enrolled for a year at Dickinson College in Carlisle, Pa., but it left her unsatisfied. The hunger to be a performer wouldn't go away. Hearing that the theater department at Boston University had a solid reputation, she transferred there. She tried hard at her courses until a smug tenured professor told her she had no talent at all.

She didn't have to take that, and she left.

Her departure from Boston University surprised her family and friends. Why was she quitting? Was young Rosie O'Donnell running away again?

They didn't understand that she'd decided to make a change in her life, and wasn't afraid at all.

CHAPTER 3

IT WAS TIME TO HIT THE ROAD, ROSIE DECIDED.

When that important professor at Boston University told her she was a total no-talent, he never suspected that his glib remark was like putting out a fire with gasoline.

He meant that she wouldn't make it in such classic dramas as those of Shakespeare or Tennessee Williams, Arthur Miller or Ibsen. And she never meant to. She intended to conquer the comedy circuit. She'd devote herself to getting experience and polishing her act in the tough world of stand-up.

"I always did it with the hopes that someone would see it and put me in a sitcom, a movie, or a Broadway show," Rosie recalled. "I never did it with aspirations of being a monologist."

She'd heard a little about the life. Aware that it might be brutal, she was willing to learn and make mistakes. Difficult as breaking into the world of comedy would be, it beat going back defeated to that sad house in Commack.

Still in her teens, Rosie went on tour, honing her act in what eventually stretched into a five-year trip through the comedy clubs of 49 states.

Almost all the other comics were older men. "Everybody was doing drugs and drinking, and I was just this little girl on the road, scared in her room," she recalled. "Time and time again, people told me to quit . . . But I didn't listen to them. I thought, 'You're all idiots!'"

Rosie refused to be discouraged by the chintzy clubs where she managed to get gigs that barely paid for cheeseburgers and two-star motel rooms. She wasn't intimidated by the hordes of competition, either. There was an army of young wanna-be comedians, all glowing with talent and dreams, hustling and bustling and vying for attention. They all had the same passionate desire to be a star.

It was the era of comedy, and hundreds of funny and not-so-funny men and women sought fame in the newly popular comedy clubs that sprang up across the country. "Saturday Night Live" had become a huge hit and launched the careers of John Belushi, Dan Aykroyd, Steve Martin, Eddie Murphy, and dozens of others. The Fox network developed a hit with "In Living Color," launching the careers of Jim Carrey and the Wayans brothers.

By the late 1980s and through the 1990s, primetime network television would finally be ready for this new crop of comedians, and build long-running, hit shows around such former stand-ups as Roseanne Barr, Ray Romano, Ellen DeGeneres, Gary Shandling, Tim Allen, Jeff Foxworthy, and, of course, Jerry Seinfeld.

Even stand-up veteran Jackie Mason would get his shot.

Comedy was becoming king.

Though these hopefuls back in 1982 and '83 were clutching for the same brass ring, the competition wasn't nasty and cutthroat. They were all in the same leaky boat defying a strong current. Rosie found there was a touching camaraderie among her fellow aspiring young comics, who all experienced the same obstacles, stumbles, and sour run-ins with arrogant and exploitive club managers. The young comics didn't let this get them down. Wryly they encouraged each other to hang in.

Rosie O'Donnell did more than that. She couldn't help it. She was a compulsive do-gooder. That's been her nature and her heritage from her mother. When she began to win a little respect on the minor league comedy circuit, she didn't hesitate to reach out to help other young stand-ups, even those who were her direct competition.

She doesn't talk much about this, but other people remember.

"She was always trying to do nice things for people," comedy club manager Louis Faranda recalled. "When some other comic wasn't getting much time on stage, she'd lobby the club boss to give that performer a better break."

She had no press agent, so the media didn't hear about her efforts to help others. She never thought her attitude was unusual. Although she was only 22, Rosie knew all too well what it meant to be down.

One day, after years on the grimy club circuit, driving from city to city in her old clunker and putting up in budget motels, Rosie took stock of her situation. The upside was there was growing opportunity and exposure for an increasing number of young female stand-ups. The downside was they were all savvy enough to have the same goal as Rosie. She decided she had to find a way, any way, to get heard above the laugh track.

In one of those accidents of fate, Ed McMahon's daughter noticed her at a comedy club and gave her the idea to try out for "Star Search," hosted by the elder McMahon. Though others held their noses up at the thought of appearing on the show, Rosie saw "Star Search" as the vehicle that could get her a little national attention.

Though her lack of success to date may have fazed lesser talents, Rosie's belief in herself and her fervor to achieve kept her true to her dream of becoming a star.

"The career advice you usually get is, 'You should quit, you're not talented enough,'" she said in an interview. "When I was on Star Search, one of the producers told the other contestants, 'She'll never be famous; she's too tough, she's too New York, and she's too heavy.' And I remember thinking, 'Gosh, he's gonna feel like a jerk when I'm famous.' Through the negativity I learned to hear myself quite loudly."

Shout it out: Rosie became comedy champion five times on "Star Search." With her winnings of more than $20,000, she made the big decision to leave the familiar surroundings of New York and move to Los Angeles to do stand-up and pursue her goal of a full-time television job.

Unlike some other aspiring funny folk, Rosie didn't depend on insult jokes and her act was a comparatively clean one. Intelligent and realistic, she had her eye on network standards and what might appeal to TV viewers and advertisers. She recognized that television served mass audiences in many parts of the country. Pleasing that great diversity of people, as well as the conservative executives who bought airtime for ad agencies, was her aim. To be a star, she knew, she would have to be fresh and funny without threatening the millions in the middle of the road.

A reviewer from the "Los Angeles Times" caught her act at the time, and wrote that Rosie "elicited big laughs early on with such bits as her observations on golf: 'I don't think golf is a sport, technically. I think golf is just men in ugly pants — walking.'

"She also took us to another side of the wild kid-dom, where four-year-old would-be comedians reside. When one of these pint-size Lenos tells a joke, 'it takes about two hours, has no semblance of order, wanders aimlessly, and YOU have to know when it's over,' O'Donnell said, and at that point she became a four-year-old monologist."

Where her routine "lost a little steam," the reviewer said, was when "she opened up her act and took a few chances on stage, primarily by interacting with the crowd. (There was, among other things, a running chat with two women sitting together, both named Betty.) And for that kind of flexibility and spontaneity, she scores major points, even if she didn't always score major laughs."

Reflecting on her stardom, Rosie told an

interviewer the secret of her success is this: "I'm relatable. When I did stand-up in little clubs in Oklahoma or Arizona, people would come up and say, 'Rosie, you're just like my friend, Eileen Murphy or Dorrie McShane' — always the Irish name."

But there were inklings even then that Rosie's future and famous moniker, The Queen of Nice, was a misnomer. With one eye on a future career in television and the other on pleasing a more sophisticated and urban clientele in the comedy clubs, Rosie pushed the envelope — in a nice way.

"Contrasted with most Improv headliners, O'Donnell incorporates a larger proportion of blue stuff and four-letter words," Duncan Strauss wrote in the "L.A. Times." "To the audience, she was the cute little kid with a foul mouth that we find endearing when we probably should be disapproving."

Rosie was onto something.

By this time, Rosie felt an increasing itch to act. She loved doing comedy, but the idea of playing roles instead of limiting herself to one liners appealed to her. She continued working the comedy clubs and looking for a savvy talent agent with the right connections who could get her some kind of TV work that paid more than "Star Search" in cash and status. Even a one-shot appearance on some ongoing series would be a big step toward stardom.

Then Rosie got that big break. Brandon Tartikoff, head of the entertainment division of NBC, caught Rosie's act at Igby's comedy club in West Los Angeles and offered her the supporting role of Maggie O'Brien, the oddball dental hygienist, in Nell Carter's popular, zany sitcom, "Gimme a Break."

Critics praised her deft performances in 11 episodes. She was funny and she was middle-of-the-road, absolutely straight-arrow every minute. She certainly didn't challenge conservative sensibilities by publicly identifying herself as a "bitch" who wasn't "nice" anymore and loved women.

That would come 15 years later, only after Rosie O'Donnell had firmly established herself as a megastar.

CHAPTER 4

THANKS TO THAT ESSENTIAL CREDENTIAL — GOOD REVIEWS FOR WORK ON A TV SHOW THAT RAN FOR A WHILE — ROSIE WAS SIGNED FOR ANOTHER TV SERIES IN 1988.

VH1's Stand-Up Spotlight was a natural for the young woman who spent her early 20s touring the dark realm of comedy clubs. She knew the young comics who would be its new kings, and as the host she got tons of laughs of her own.

She was on her way, everyone told her.

No one mentioned her by now obvious weight problem. The country was becoming more fanatical about health and fitness by the month, but people in the television business and audiences accepted Rosie O'Donnell as a cheerful, chubby, and cute entertainer — the fresh-faced alter ego of the equally rotund, wisecracking and world-weary Roseanne Barr.

Rosie would later, in typical fashion, announce that the world's most disgusting four-letter word was "diet."

"I'm not going to diet again," the comedian

proclaimed. "I'm tired of this ridiculous preoccupation American women have for their weight," she told a friend. "It's all for men! It's a male conspiracy!"

Entertainer was what she wanted to be — star entertainer.

So what if the pounds kept coming? Who was counting? If other women her age were eating Snackwells and downing Slimfasts to conform to the new standard of slim, trim and healthy, Rosie countered with arguments about the dangers of excess weight loss.

Often when people have problems, they swiftly find nice ways and cozy words to keep from facing them. Sugar-coating our problems makes it easier to avoid doing anything about them. Advancing into the TV world she'd fantasized about for so long, Rosie denied the danger of her huge weight gain by thinking of herself as big-boned or plump.

But as with millions of others, Rosie's struggle with her weight has always been an issue of mind over matter.

"Whenever anyone tells me to lose weight, I always laugh, like I could, but I'm just keeping it on because I like to!" she once joked. "But when I'm at my thinnest, I never really feel thin, and when I'm at my heaviest, I'm always surprised at how I got there."

She knew the reasons she was overweight: Her bulk kept others at an emotional distance, plus she had a deep-seated fear stemming from her mother's wasting away that equated thinness with death. She knew the reasons she was heavy, but for almost her entire life she has teetered between wanting to lose weight and simply accepting herself as she is.

"I stuggle with it every day," she admitted in late 1997. "And when I read in the newspaper that some radio jock says, 'She's so fat and gross,' it hurts my feelings. I sometimes get out of the shower and think, 'Oh, boy, I have to do something.' And then I have to work hard to stand in front of the mirror after that image goes through and say, 'This is who you are, and this is where you are. You're okay in this body, and you're a great, healthy, loveable, and loving person, and go forward with love.' And that's what I try to do. I just try to accept myself for where I am."

Back in 1988, however, she had only her meteoric career to think about. Her focus was on the here and now, not on the responsibilities that might come with raising children some time or other.

The following year, Rosie co-starred in "Pair of Jokers," and in 1991, she added her special humor to the cult favorite cartoon "Ren and Stimpy." Rosie's public reputation grew steadily with each new television show.

In 1992, she co-starred with Melissa Gilbert in Fox's "Stand by Your Man." She played Lorraine Popowski, and Gilbert played Rochelle Dunphy. They were two sisters who married the wrong men. One guy was an embezzler, and the other a two-bit con man. The series revolved around the sisters' adventures as they waited for their husbands to get out on parole. The show wasn't a hit, but it was the perfect vehicle for Rosie, letting her hone her scene-stealing prowess for the film career that was to follow.

Penny Marshall, who was directing the movie "A League of Their Own," about female teams playing professional baseball during World War II when many men were off to war, had her eyes on Rosie.

"She called my agent to ask if I could play baseball," Rosie recalled, "and from then on I had a movie career."

Rosie read the script and decided she would do anything to have the part of Doris Murphy. "I thought, 'If I don't get this part, I'll quit show business,'" Rosie recalled. "If there's one thing I can do better than Meryl Streep and Glenn Close, it's play baseball." She jokingly recalled that when the other kids were choosing up sides for sandlot baseball games, "I was always the first girl picked. I got picked ahead of my three brothers, which I think still affects them."

Though the part was written for "a hot, sexy girl," director Marshall says she liked Rosie so much "we changed the story to suit her. She can make anything funny."

Joining stars Madonna, Geena Davis and Tom Hanks in the movie, Rosie got the role of Doris Murphy, a third basewoman with the mouth of a truck driver. The spunky, funky, chunky Doris wasn't the biggest role in the film, but every reviewer noticed Rosie. Joe Brown of the "Washington Post" wrote, "Madonna made the team. So did Oscar winner Geena Davis. But the MVP of 'A League of Their Own' ... is unquestionably comedian Rosie O'Donnell."

It's now the stuff of legend how Madonna stipulated that she meet Rosie in a will-we-get-along informal audition before filming.

Both were gifted, savvy entertainers, and both were independent, irreverent, and almost fearless.

Madonna had already enslaved the ever news hungry media people by going where she wanted, doing what she wanted, and saying anything that came to her mind. Freedom and fun were her rules. Her fame already established, Madonna accepted the younger Rosie as a cool sister figure and friend.

The fact that Rosie was one of the few members of the nearly all female cast who could actually play baseball helped. The two powerhouse women bonded on the field when the cameras were rolling and at night when they went out dining, drinking, and talking dogs, diets and deals.

Rosie says she had idolized Madonna and was terrified when she met her for the first time. "Totally," she said in an interview. "Had diarrhea." But she took the bull by the horns and reached out to an immediate connection with the Material Girl, citing Madonna's recent semi-autobiographical movie "Truth or Dare." "I looked her in the eye and said, 'My mom died when I was ten, too. Your movie reminded me a lot of my life.' And that was it. We became friends right then."

They soon both had chihuahuas, one male and the other female, and tried to breed them. They shared a fondness for the lush life in sophisticated Miami Beach, too, and Rosie made an offer when Madonna put her deluxe mansion on the market. Always a perfectionist, Rosie wanted certain repairs before signing the big bucks contract. That turned Madonna off, and the deal fell apart.

Rosie and Madonna didn't. They remained warm, noisy friends. Though Madonna knew Rosie didn't want advice and avoided exercise like the plague, she couldn't help urging her plump pal to diet and do more workouts. Ms. O'Donnell declined in her usual boisterous fashion.

"Won't do it," she told a reporter. "That's her. I'm me. She sleeps with her trainer and I ignore mine."

Madonna, who had a child with her trainer, Carlos Leon, before moving onto another marriage with movie producer Guy Ritchie, laughed. The two remained so close that Rosie would eventually name Madonna her first son Parker's godmother.

A League of Their Own was a grand slam for Rosie, bringing in one movie offer after another. In 1993, she worked with Tom Hanks and Meg Ryan in the blockbuster romantic comedy "Sleepless in Seattle." Rosie played Becky, sidekick and editor to Ryan's newspaper reporter Annie Reed.

Like Penny Marshall, Sleepless director Nora Ephron was taken with Rosie's natural ease. "The audience looks at her and thinks, I wish that could be my best friend," Ephron said. "Rosie had that in Sleepless, and it's why her show works. She's a fantastically open person."

Rosie, ever searching for her mother, in return found another surrogate in Ephron, as she had in Bernice Ellard from the old neighborhood.

"Nora's a mother to me," Rosie said. "She's the one I go to when I have questions."

Happy for a high-profile role in a hit movie, Rosie couldn't help but offer an honest critique of the film itself. Though she has said the film remains her favorite on-screen effort, Rosie of all people knew what it was like to lose a mother at a young age. She admitted that she thought the film's story line, in which a 9-year-old boy almost immediately gets over the death of his mother and tries to find a new mate for his dad, highly improbable. She and Meg "would be hysterical laughing at the film," she said in 1993. "It was ridiculous."

"New York Newsday" said of the movie, "Rosie O'Donnell has the bulk of the best one-liners, and her performance is a joy."

That same year she appeared in "Another Stakeout," a sequel to the 1987 Stakeout cop drama starring Richard Dreyfuss. Rosie did her best as Assistant District Attorney Garrett, working with a small dog and even a smaller script.

Despite reviewers universally panning "Another Stakeout," Rosie rushed back onto a sound stage in Exit to Eden, a film released in 1994. Described as a "strange cinematic catastrophe" by critic Leonard Maltin, the movie followed two cops, played by Dan Aykroyd and Rosie, as they infiltrated a sadomasochistic fantasy camp. To play detective Sheila Kingston, Rosie had to lose enough weight to squeeze into the leather outfit of a dominatrix. She gave it her all and weighed in at a svelte 150.

"O'Donnell's bright performance is the one justification for its [the movie's] existence," commented Maltin.

Rosie, however, would later complain that one night upon stumbling across a rerun of Exit to Eden, "I was full of shame and embarrassment. It was so bad I had to turn it off. I was having an anxiety attack and I needed a Xanax. I didn't look good at all. I was horrible. And I was in that outfit! What was I thinking?"

In another interview, she admitted she accepted the part only because "I wanted to tell people I took the role Sharon Stone turned down. I couldn't believe that at some big Hollywood meeting someone said, 'Hmmmm, can't get Sharon stone? Let's get Rosie O'Donnell!'"

The small art film in which Rosie next appeared garnered even more dismal reviews. "Now and Then" had an ambitious script, a cast that included Demi Moore and Melanie Griffith, and a swift trip to video stores.

✽✽✽✽✽

Movies and stardom weren't all Rosie had on her mind that year.

Neither the media nor her growing ranks of fans had been paying too much attention to Rosie's love life. But by the time Rosie was playing Gina Barrisano in "Beautiful Girls," filmed in 1995 for release in 1996, Hollywood insiders were starting to whisper — the rising star had made a new friend, and her name was Michelle Blakely.

Between movie jobs, Rosie had come to Broadway and jumped at the chance to perform in the musical "Grease." That's where she met her new and very close acquaintance, Michelle, the trim and accomplished stage veteran who was co-starring in the production. Soon Rosie and Michelle were deeply involved, and most of the "Grease" ensemble knew that Michelle had moved into Rosie's comfortable Manhattan apartment.

It was no big deal to the Broadway community,

who'd historically welcomed gay men into its fold and whose gay women were becoming more visible by the last quarter of the 20th century. And the film and television sophisticates in California barely batted an eyelash when they heard talk that Rosie was half of a caring couple back East.

Along with her newfound love and fame and money, there was something even more special on Rosie's mind — she was about to become a mother — and, though she didn't know it then, a household name.

CHAPTER 5

"CUTIE PATOOTIE," AS ROSIE REFERS TO HER FIRST SON PARKER O'DONNELL (AND NUMEROUS OTHER DESERVING ADORABLE TYKES), ARRIVED TO LIGHT UP THE STAR'S LIFE IN 1995. THE PRIVATE ADOPTION HAD BEEN ARRANGED THROUGH A LAWYER. ON THE DAY THE MOTHER DELIVERED, ROSIE WAS IN HER OWN HOME, DOWN ON HER KNEES SCRUBBING THE FLOOR.

The social worker telephoned Rosie to report a development she hadn't anticipated, and it wasn't simply that the baby had come a few days early. She knew that Rosie believed that God wanted her to have a girl.

"Is there a problem?" Rosie blurted out uneasily.

"No problem," the embarrassed social worker assured her while taking a deep breath. "You have a healthy son."

Rosie was silent for a moment. "I had dead mother stuff to work out," she acknowledged in "Find Me." "Surely, my life lessons would be learned through my daughter. What would I do with a boy?"

It took her two seconds to know the answer — love him intensely and raise him well.

"Any questions?" the social worker asked.

"Yeah," practical Rosie O'Donnell replied. "When is he coming home?"

The boy she named Parker spent his first night in the hospital. He was tiny and perfect, his proud mother recalls, and he slept like, well, a baby. Rosie, on the other hand, was up all night. When morning arrived, she was red-eyed, pacing the floor in the hopeful excitement of the love beyond words that a woman feels for her prayed-for first child.

She watched out the window for the Volvo station wagon that would bring him. It was blue, the same color as the less upscale station wagon the O'Donnells had back in Commack. When he finally arrived, the social worker rang the doorbell and gave a wet-eyed Rosie a very small yellow blanket. A patch of the most beautiful matted black hair Rosie ever saw was sticking up from it. When her son was in her arms, he suddenly and right on time opened his blue eyes to stare into hers.

"Hi, Mama," she thought instantly. "Here we go."

Rosie had always known she would one day be a mother. "I always knew I would have children," she said. "It was never a question, just as I knew what I wanted for my career, I knew I would be a mother. And though I was not against being a birth mother, this opportunity came up. I knew people who had adopted, so I put myself on a list, like throwing a wish into the air. I thought, 'If this is meant to be, then it will happen.'"

It happened — but like any new mother, there was

plenty to learn. As when she had her first period, and at other times during the awkward years, when Rosie held tiny Parker in her arms she found herself desperately missing her own mother.

"The time I missed her the most in my adult life was the first night that I had Parker," she recalled. "I was up at 3 a.m. and he was not drinking the bottle. I was scared and wished that my mom was there to tell me, 'He's going to survive and so will you.' After he fell asleep, I was crying hard, thinking, God, I really ache to have her here."

There were other travails common to first-time motherhood — especially given that her first child was a boy.

"I was singularly unprepared for a son," she admitted. "I read all these books on adoption and I didn't have any help, because I wanted it to be just him and me." But she learned a lesson one day when actresses Rita Wilson and Kate Capshaw dropped by to see Parker.

"Rita went to change his diaper," Rosie recalled. "She said, 'Why didn't you have him circumcised?' I said, 'Look, here are the adoption papers, they say he's circumcised.' And Rita holds up the baby and says, 'Well, look at this — he's not circumcised.'"

"Now," Rosie added, "I know this sounds crazy, because I grew up with three brothers. But I never saw my brothers naked when we were kids. And because my mom died when I was young, she was never around to talk about those things. Call me silly. I became hysterical, uncontrollable. But Rita and Kate took care of it. They called a doctor friend who is also a mohel (a trained Jewish official who performs circumcisions). He came over the next day and circumcised the baby. Kate brought bagels and lox — we had a little party!"

The lonely young woman from Commack had yearned for motherhood for a long time. "I think all motherless children feel that having their own children will fill that hole in their lives," she confessed.

Plus, she added, "One of the great things about having children is you get to right the wrongs of your childhood. It's a wonderful chance to give yourself what you didn't have by giving it to your kid."

Motherhood is still one of the most dominant aspects of her personality. Her children are of enormous importance and joy to motherless Rosie O'Donnell, who is acutely aware of her vital responsibilities as a parent.

She has been — from the minute her first child arrived — a completely dedicated mother. She may have some diva in her in terms of the world of entertainment, but in the house she's an unpretentious mother who'll do whatever it takes to raise healthy, happy and down-to-earth children.

Becoming a mother also brought her full-circle with her own mother, and helped close the open wound that had troubled Rosie since she was 10 years old.

"When he looks at me, I can finally see my own mother as a woman, not just as my mom," she said of baby Parker. "I feel closer to her than I have in a long time. I finally understand just how much she loved me. I realize that she felt, for me, the things I feel for him."

And having a child helped Rosie's own state of

mind, always tortured before by the sense of loss her mother's death left.

"Before him, I was a little depressed," she admitted in an interview. "I knew I wasn't as happy as I thought I should be, based on my success. But when I'm with him, I feel true joy."

"It's been very, very healing for me," Rosie said of motherhood. "For the first time, I can perceive my mother as an adult. My images of her were always idealized. I never really saw her as a woman. But when I first held my son in my arms, I had that overwhelming connection and a feeling of immense love that I never had before. I thought, 'My mom felt this for me. And for my siblings.' So it was really an emotional time for me, those first few months with Parker, to connect with my mom and to think of her as a woman and not as my little girl image of her."

Rosie's life changed forever the day she held Parker in her arms for the first time. Suddenly, a movie career wasn't so important. She quickly found she hated to be away from her son for even a moment. She tried bringing him with her to the set — only to find that was no solution. "I was tired of trying to play with him between takes, and having to make sure he didn't throw up on my costumes," she said.

It wasn't long before the distance between Manhattan and Hollywood began to trouble Rosie. The completion of filming in 1995 of the films "Beautiful Girls" and "Harriet the Spy" gave her an opportunity to make an important decision. Even before these movies headed to the theaters for their modest runs, she made up her mind to drastically reduce her work in feature films, which took her away from home in Manhattan for weeks at a time and kept her separated from Parker. That decision was further sealed when she came home from filming "Harriet the Spy" to find that little Parker wouldn't have anything to do with her.

Rosie's rising success in television and films had earned her representation by a major talent agency. She told the executive who handled her bookings to get her steady work in New York on a long-term basis.

The agent did his job. Working with Warner Television, he put together a talk show for her. It was to be called "The Rosie O'Donnell Show."

Premiering in the summer of 1996, in the age of the outrageous "Jerry Springer Show" and its ilk, Rosie had a vision for the show that harkened back to a simpler time.

"I'm trying to bring back the kind of show that I grew up watching — the kind of show that brought entertainers that I loved into my living room each day, the kind of show that I could watch with my grandmother and my little sister, and everyone got something out of it," she said. "I don't think I'm trying to save TV, or be the antithesis of sleaze TV shows. I'm just trying to do Merv Griffin for the '90s, and I genuinely have an appreciation of celebrities, of talent, of musicals. It's genuine. My agenda is just to make a fun, entertaining family show that you can watch generationally in your house."

She was to be star, host and executive producer. It was expensive, and it was a hard sell, but the big-time syndication company agreed to roll the dice. The show was to be pure Rosie — from top to bottom

— five days a week in the Big Apple, with her in charge of everything.

The syndication company was also to pay her a salary of several million dollars a year, and commit many millions more to the whole package.

The stations across the country that signed on had no guarantee that this roly-poly graduate of stand-up would come through as the heart of a daily talk show. Nobody else in television could be sure, either. The only one who knew she had a sure-fire hit in the making was Rosie O'Donnell herself.

She had to do this for her son, Parker — and for another kid — that middle child whose time had come to be a star.

CHAPTER 6

WITH UNABASHED CANDOR, ROSIE O'DONNELL
DECLARES THAT HER SON HAS "BROUGHT HER TO A NEW
LEVEL OF LOVING, BEYOND THE BEYOND."
And it was in this state of mind she began her
challenging daily TV show. Unwilling to be separated
from her son, she persuaded the production
company to help set up a playpen area at her office
where a nanny could keep an eye on Parker. Rosie
understood that she'd have to be careful so her son
wouldn't be a spoiled rich brat, but she also knew
that having him near her was good for him.

Rosie had two rules for the show. The first one was
to be nice to the rich and famous celebrities who
agreed to appear on the show. The second rule was
she was dead-set on not exploiting young Parker,
though he toddled just feet away from the desk at
which his famous mom sat while hosting the show.

Referring to the high-profile childhoods of the
offspring of Cher and, especially, Kathie Lee Gifford,
Rosie said: "I don't want him to become like Chastity

Bono or Cody Gifford where his name and experiences are public record."

But don't think her happiness with her son made her a softie on the set. She knew exactly what she wanted the show to be, and she was ruthless in fulfilling that vision.

In the first six months of the show, Rosie fired more than 30 of her show's staff members. Network TV jobs pay extremely well, so people have to meet high performance standards. If they don't cut it or don't get along well with the powers that be, they can be fired faster than a channel surfer hits the remote. If the star wants you to leave, you're gone.

Even before the first broadcast of "The Rosie O'Donnell Show," everyone associated with the production knew that the senior producers and Ms. O'Donnell were the ones calling the shots. The show had originally been staffed by production executives who hired hip, energetic, young people who had some television experience. That's the way TV series are generally launched.

But Rosie wasn't satisfied with what was being done for the series that carried her name. She felt her reputation was at a stake. She fired one director, three producers, writers, heads of research, her stage manager, a guest coordinator, and other staffers. The exodus was larger than at any other show launched in 1996.

And, causing some controversy when word leaked out, Rosie replaced them all with women.

Some of those who got the boot angrily described the star as "a master of belittling and lambasting," claiming that she often "humiliated" people at staff meetings.

"Rosie has everyone quaking with fear before staff meetings," disclosed one show insider. "She sits at the head of the table and bellows 'I gotta have ideas. If anyone expects to pick up their paycheck, they better speak up now. I can't hear you! What've we got here, a room full of mice, or just idiots?' She has a habit of picking things up and throwing them while she's having a little fit. It doesn't matter to her if the object just misses someone."

Said another ex-employee, "And the irony is that after suffering through the agony of constantly being humiliated at staff meetings or during production, it's almost a relief getting fired!"

Whether Rosie was excessively harsh is debatable, given that TV is an industry where it's not unusual for defenseless employees to be ridiculed or cursed.

It's fair to say that her standards were high, and Rosie was demanding, tough, bluntly critical and, at times, impetuous. She has proved she owns an infectious, cutting wit, demonstrating this for years in her stand-up act, but no host of a daily TV talk show could be expected to generate enough lively chatter to feed such a monster. Every host has found it essential to work with a team of writers. Getting the best team has challenged all of them.

The talk in the trade is that Rosie expected writers to prove themselves immediately — if not sooner. At first meetings with a potential writer, she would say, "OK. Be funny. You've got 45 seconds."

That shook up a lot of them, though people who know Rosie say it might have been expected. They argue that she didn't mean to be abusive, but as a high-powered diva she wanted perfection for the show with her name on it. She could be merciless in criticizing writers — both those who worked for her and those who desperately wanted to — but she paid them huge salaries and gave them generous vacations.

The way Rosie dominated the staff and just about every decision made about the show didn't win her any brownie points with many pros in network television, but they knew that the star of any hit show can be a total monarch. As long as the ratings are good, the syndicator won't meddle with whatever the star does, because the diva on duty is the reason people watch and advertisers pay.

That was definitely true with "The Rosie O'Donnell Show."

More and more people across North America tuned in, and the advertising revenues soon followed. Rosie was reported by some journalists to be earning an annual income of $3 million. In fact, she earned a whopping $20 million a year.

Whether she was the Queen of Nice, as "Newsweek" famously hailed her (she told her publicist at the time that that nickname was certain to come back and "bite me in the ass"), or a royal bitch, she earned every penny she got. She worked like a Trojan, using all her talents and bringing onto the show her many friends, all stars in theater, television and Hollywood.

Unlike many other talk-show demigods, Rosie gave her energy and air time to more than just the obligatory patter with celebrities sent by their studios to plug their latest movie or CD. She cared about many causes and people, and she exuberantly invited her viewers to join her in supporting "the good ones."

She again credited her success with her own "relatable" persona, harking back to her stand-up days when clubgoers would tell her how much she reminded them of people they knew. "Everybody had a sister or a best friend like me, and that same non-threatening feeling goes into the show because a lot of women are competitive and our show is more of a celebration," she said.

But not everything went right that first season. Rosie found herself in a bizarre situation during the show's first week when one of her idols, the former teeny-bopper sensation Donny Osmond, poked fun at her weight when he saw Rosie had pulled out all of her childhood Donny memorablia as a tribute to his appearance.

"It was the first week of the show and I don't think he had seen it before," Rosie said. "He's on the road doing Joseph and the Amazing Technicolor Dreamcoat. I believe that when he came out and saw my albums and my Donny Osmond doll, he thought I was going to ridicule him.

"Instead of seeing what I was doing as a reverential tribute — which it was, because I honestly do like Donny Osmond and his music, and I have the doll — I think he thought I was going to be aggressively poking fun at him. So what happened was, I was saying, 'Oh, Donny, you have to go and do this dangerous stunt out in Utah, and God, I'm worried about you. You know what, don't go on the helicopter. I'll go and be your stuntperson, I'll be your double, and I'll do it for you.'

"And he said, 'I don't think the helicopter can handle that much weight.' So I took a moment and went, 'Whoooa!' That comment became the bane of his existence, because everywhere he went people were saying, 'How could you?' And I didn't let up on it. The next day, I went on the show and I said, 'Can you believe Donny Osmond called me fat?' I think anyone who has ever had their weight be an issue in their life felt the pain of having lived through that.

"I don't believe it was necessarily malicious — it was just stupid of him. I think he thought that this would be his shot and that because I'm a comic, I could take it. He did apologize profusely during the commercial, and afterward."

Booed for weeks afterward wherever he went, Donny agreed to come back and do his penance to the new Queen of Daytime Television. "I made him put on a puppy-dog suit and sing Puppy Love," she said. "It was the highest-rated show ever."

Rosie's good-time, good-clean-fun formula was making her rich. And the intense woman who has said more than once that in a basic sense her life froze at age 10, when her mother died, began to show she is first and foremost committed to a huge number of groups and programs that help children.

It is difficult to name any other entertainer who has given so much — on the air and off — to help children. She has been amazingly generous in promoting a wide range of child-oriented philanthropies on her program, and nobody has appeared at more benefits to raise money for children's organizations. Just about every month, she proudly shows up at such events to do her part — and pulls in other celebrities whose glamorous presence will generate ticket sales and income for the children. Rosie also puts her own money where her mouth is.

How much money?

Seven million dollars.

That's the figure the girl who grew up in the house with generic-brand everything gladly gave to help children during the six years she reigned supreme on the national airwaves.

"I think my activism came from my childhood," she said, in explaining her generosity and her goal of helping children. "I grew up in a home that was not ideal. We were neglected in many ways. I always knew that I had an affinity for children, and I had a desire to touch and inspire them in the way that entertainers touched and inspired and provided me solace in a less than happy childhood.

"When I was a kid, Barbra Streisand was the most famous person to me, the person I most wanted to be. When my mother was sick, I thought, 'If Barbra Streisand's mother had cancer and everyone sent in a dollar, they'd find a cure.' At nine years old, I knew that with fame comes the power to change society — to cure diseases, to help people. When my mother died, I felt powerless — like there was nothing I could do to help. Now, I feel there are things I can do."

Broadway was her other baby. She never got over her passion for the Great White Way, and the theater community has blessed her every day for her on-air raves about shows that sold so many tickets. Rosie's enthusiasm for many productions — especially musicals, which she's reveled in since her mother introduced her to glorious show tunes that have become American standards — has filled tens of thousands of live theater seats with young and old alike.

Ever loyal and true to her crowd, she said she bucked Warners by inviting her Broadway friends on her show. "In the beginning, Warners didn't want me to do theater guests on the show," she said. "But I grew up wanting to be Bette Midler and Barbra Streisand, and to me there's nothing better than sitting in that audience with the waxy Playbill in your hand and the lights go down and the music goes up and it's kind of overwhelming."

Rosie was soon so strongly identified with Broadway theater that she was asked to host the national telecast of the Antoinette Perry Awards. The "Tony Awards," as they're known, are the equivalent of the Oscars for the stage, and they had been struggling to win TV viewers. That was no problem the night hot Rosie O'Donnell was the saucy, savvy and dynamic host.

That first year of "The Rosie O'Donnell Show" brought Rosie accolades from every corner of the entertainment world. Though some wondered at her choice of guests, which seemed to lean toward lightweights, Rosie defended the sappy, happy-talk tone of the show.

"People like Steve Lawrence and Eydie Gorme, I love them," she said. "The Captain and Tennille, they were a part of my childhood, and I'm not going to take a shot at them. Having Florence Henderson on or Julie Andrews singing from The Sound of Music — those are significant emotional moments for me. We're an afternoon talk show with a largely female audience. We're not late-night, we're not edgy."

Viewers responded to what had to have been, for most of its run, the safest talk show on television — "Merv Griffin for the '90s" was what Rosie had in mind, and it was what she gave us.

She coupled her wild television success with her deep joy at home. Her son was growing into a delightful little boy. Her loving companion, Michelle Blakely, was happy to be with both of them.

To paraphrase a Stephen Sondheim lyric, everything was coming up Rosies. Nothing could go wrong.

Then something did.

CHAPTER 7

AT CHRISTMAS 1996, MICHELLE BLAKELY WAS HAPPY TO BE 20-MONTH-OLD PARKER'S CO-MOTHER AND ROSIE'S PARTNER — SO HAPPY, IN FACT, THAT SHE FELT IT WAS TIME FOR HER AND HER PARTNER TO TAKE THEIR RELATIONSHIP TO THE NEXT LEVEL. THE TRIM AND PRETTY 32-YEAR-OLD SINGER-DANCER-ACTRESS HAD MADE A NAME ON STAGE AND IN TELEVISION. NOW, LIKE MANY WOMEN HER AGE, SHE WANTED TO GET MARRIED.

To Rosie O'Donnell, and in public.

Rosie didn't want to marry Michelle. She wasn't ready to do that. Insiders believe that there was sincere love between the two, but there was also something else that separated them. A friend of the couple confided to a reporter that the star feared such a marriage would "kill" her in Middle America.

She might have been right. The truth is, even now the big television audience might be uncomfortable with such a wedding. And the fact is, a number of gay women and men in Hollywood continue to live in the closet, concerned that being "outed" could forever ruin their careers. Such fears that kept stars such as Rock Hudson forever quiet about his sexual preferences still encourage some in show business and many other fields to be less-than-candid about their personal lives.

And it's not like the fears are unfounded. When the talented actress-comedian Ellen DeGeneres, star of the TV sitcom "Ellen," elected to go public with the "news" that she was, indeed, a lesbian, a chunk of her public elected to switch the channel. It was after Rosie decided that a marriage to Blakely was way ahead of U.S. public opinion that DeGeneres chose to end the rumors and confirm her preference and lifestyle.

Out of the closet, the show's focus switched from Ellen's quirky friends and her own Lucille Ball-like foibles to Ellen's new, openly gay world. Whether viewers were turned off because one of their favorite TV characters had been revealed to be a lesbian, or because the show simply became a vehicle for gay rights and just wasn't funny anymore — and the truth probably rests somewhere in between — the fact remains that her ratings quickly declined. Unhappy network executives pulled the plug on her series. Those still in the closet, as Rosie was, sat up and took notice.

Even after the demise of her own show, Ellen DeGeneres herself was reportedly urging Rosie to come out of the closet. "Ellen told Rosie, 'What's the big deal?'" said one close insider. "'Do you think you're fooling anyone?' But Rosie replied, 'I have major endorsements. I have movie contracts and children's book deals — these people will not understand.'"

But Ellen persisted. She told Rosie, "We in the business all know you're gay. Join me and 'fess up. It's good for all of us. I'm not hiding anything anymore. People get the real me."

"But Rosie is so afraid of coming out that she canceled an autobiography she was going to write," the source confided. 'She returned the $2 million advance and told the publishers she couldn't do it — she wasn't ready."

And Rosie wasn't ready for Michelle's next demand, either. It turned out marriage wasn't all she wanted. Rosie, with her multimillion-dollar income, had been supporting both of them, shelling out for rent, food — even her companion's wardrobe. Blakely might have been uneasy about the future if for any reason the relationship ended.

Michelle wanted galimony — that's what well-connected sources called it.

According to them, Michelle had requested a written agreement assuring that Rosie would take care of her financially whether they stayed together or not. Many male stars and executives signed palimony contracts with their female intimates. Why couldn't gay women?

The syndicators of "The Rosie O'Donnell Show" went ballistic at the prospect of Rosie openly marrying a woman and signing a galimony agreement. So shaken by this possible threat to their great cash cow were they that even though they well knew how fiercely independent Rosie was, and how short her fuse, they made their acute concern clear to her.

And what was Rosie's response to the "galimony" and marriage request? "Rosie freaked," a source said.

"It was like a knife piercing Michelle's loving heart."

Friends of the sad couple saw how unhappy they were that December. They recognized that Blakely was deeply hurt by this rejection and that Rosie, although she didn't want to marry Michelle, didn't want to hurt or lose her. They meant a lot to each other, and the star was distressed when her intimate companion decided to move on with her life and found a separate apartment in Manhattan.

"Michelle was heartbroken and Rosie's a basket case," an insider said. "They both loved each other very much and wanted to work it out. It was the saddest Christmas and New Year for both of them."

"Rosie supported Michelle, like a traditional husband takes care of a wife," the source explained. "She paid for all the food, bought all her clothes, looked after all her needs. They were like a married couple."

"But Michelle wasn't content to bathe in someone else's success," the source confided. "Michelle no longer wanted to be mate to the queen of daytime TV. She's a proud, talented singer, dancer and actress. She's been in Broadway shows and TV movies. She put her career on hold to be Rosie's lover and companion."

But the source said Michelle worried that if the relationship soured, she'd wind up being tossed aside "like a used Kleenex."

She told the source, "I'm very, very sad. But there was no other way. My life was going nowhere. I love Parker like he was my own child and I miss him every moment of every day."

Then 34 years old, Rosie took emotional refuge in

her work. She was doing an excellent show, but she wasn't doing quite as good a job controlling her tensions. She's spoken frankly of her years of therapy accompanied by prescribed medication. This route is not at all unusual among entertainment leaders, be they executives or divas, and friends say it helped Rosie — but perhaps not quite enough.

Rosie O'Donnell has publicly said that rage is a basic contributor to comedy and has stood firm in her confession. It's not a crime, but she's got a temper. She's had it for a long time. Stars and tycoons don't have to hide it, and Rosie has been suppressing it less in recent years.

"The Rosie O'Donnell Show" was holy to her. It was a dream come true for the enormously gifted and driven star, and she protected it ferociously. Like other stars with their own talk shows, Rosie had both a large economic interest in it and a whopper of an ego investment.

Shortly after Michelle left, Rosie's temper was sorely tested. She was supposed to appear with a bunch of other celebrities on a TV special celebrating the 65th birthday of movie legend Elizabeth Taylor. The event was to raise cash to care for AIDS patients, the broadcast was set for early 1997, and Rosie promised to be there.

Then the Queen of Nice sent word she couldn't come. This was a big disappointment to the event planners, who were baffled, since anyone who watched Rosie's show was aware that one of her top philanthropic interests was gay women and men who had been discriminated against.

According to an inside source, the hush-hush

reason Rosie pulled out of the birthday tribute was that Taylor had postponed a scheduled appearance on Rosie's show. Her people had sent word to Rosie's senior producers that Taylor would have to be in the hospital for major surgery at the time, and the talk was that she urgently needed a brain operation.

Furious since they had promoted Rosie's appearance at the gala event, the Taylor team took to the telephone to make threats.

Nobody in either camp has given a public explanation, but in the end Rosie did participate. She did so electronically, however, not in person. A taped spot of Rosie was aired on the birthday show.

Rosie's certainly not the first talk-show host to be furious when an important guest cancels or postpones a scheduled appearance. Some irate hosts have been known to bar the offender from ever appearing on the show in the future.

Rosie was also incensed when Joan Rivers mocked her on national TV. The diva didn't stop at merely barring Rivers from her show forever, but continued the battle even after "The Rosie O'Donnell Show" ended. In a big-ticket casino show Rosie sneered that Rivers was, due to plastic surgery, looking "like an alien."

To insiders, the star wars came as no surprise.

At home, of course, Rosie's language wasn't anything like that. She was careful in raising her son, who, one family friend joked, wasn't just the apple of Rosie's eye, but the whole orchard.

Before they split up, Rosie and Michelle had recruited an excellent nanny for Parker. About 40, trim, and with short blonde hair, the attractive Kate Fitzgerald had some stage experience as well as good references in child care. She got along well with the boy.

Unlike other rich, busy and famous women, Rosie did not leave the lad's upbringing to an employee, however. She loved Parker much too much, and she made sure that she spent a lot of quality time with him every day. She was with him when he awakened, and read him to sleep every night. She made a point of getting home from the studio as soon as she could each afternoon.

Rosie was committed to being with Parker whenever he might need her, and not miss any of the important moments of his growing up from toddler to strong active boy. She was determined not to leave him with any sense of being less than other boys his age. He'd be off to school soon, and she didn't want him to be troubled by the fact he had no father.

Rosie was smart enough to understand that attention and caring were more important than the money she could devote to him. Having herself grown up with a sense of something vital missing during her essentially parentless adolescence, Rosie didn't want him to feel inferior to boys who had a father at home.

On her show and in her stand-up act, Rosie made no secret of her opinion that Edward O'Donnell did a miserable job as her father. Her conviction that he had shortchanged her was obvious when, in the course of on-camera conversations with guests, she'd find some reason — inner hurt, no doubt — to suddenly remark that her father was an "idiot" and a heavy drinker. "The head of the Irish drinking people," she proclaimed him.

Becoming a mother didn't mellow her enough to forgive her father for all of his shortcomings, whether real or imagined by Rosie.

She continued to cut herself off from her father, who had remarried, retired, and moved to North Carolina. Though she carried the precious memories of her mother with her every day, she held deep bitterness in her heart for Edward O'Donnell and what she remembered as his emotional distance in the years following the elder Roseann O'Donnell's death.

When Edward had open-heart surgery in the fall of 1995, said a family source, all of Rosie's siblings were either with him or called and sent flowers, but Rosie was a no-show and remained aloof. Though she'd made him the butt of her jokes for years, Edward "hadn't realized how bitter she was toward him until then," the insider revealed.

"He could have died on the operating table. All of Rosie's siblings were there or sent flowers, but Rosie didn't bother to see him. He told me later, 'I wish I knew why she hates me so much.' It eats him up inside that Rosie hasn't come to North Carolina for a visit to show off Parker.

"It's just a shame. Rosie's missing a lot. And so is Parker. That little boy needs grandparents. But Rosie acts like she could care less."

Some in the family blamed the psychiatrists Rosie had seen over the years for her bitter feelings toward her dad.

"She's been in therapy her entire adult life," one insider said. "Psychiatrists make you think every problem you have in life is your parents' fault. She's been brainwashed by some shrink to think Ed was a bad father. It's hard for many in the family to understand, since we've known him as a straight shooter who worked hard to support his kids after their mom died."

Although a pack of journalists went looking for the seemingly despicable Edward O'Donnell as his daughter's fame grew and "Rosie" became a household word, a brand, and a foundation, it was only the Enquirer that found him in retirement. He wasn't bitter about his estrangement from Rosie or what she said about him to millions of strangers on her talk show.

He did not want to get into a public spat with his famous daughter. "What does our relationship have to do with anything?" was all he would say.

Is it possible the other O'Donnell children had a very different recollection of their past? There's another puzzling question raised by the insider, who insists that Ed O'Donnell wasn't a terrible and ungiving parent at all.

Is it possible that her psychotherapists turned Rosie O'Donnell against her father during her years of therapy?

Was she brainwashed to believe things that were not true?

A number of courts have recognized that false memories might be implanted by mental health specialists trying to treat people. In some nationally covered cases of alleged child abuse, the ugly accusations have been overturned on this basis. It's still a controversial issue.

Since Rosie began speaking about some sort of unspecified abuse during her youth, people in and out of show business have speculated whether she meant verbal abuse or was hinting at a never discussed physical battering.

Or was the whole thing in her mind?

Not getting emotional support from a parent can be hurtful, but does it fit the generally accepted definition of abuse? A psychotherapist — and Rosie has seen more than one in the last 20 years — might believe that the term should include starving a child of affection, even though there's plenty of food on the table.

Rosie has tried to mitigate her harsh comments about her father, claiming they're all made in fun. "The stuff about my dad is all made up," she once said. "Your job as a comedian is to take a point, exaggerate it, and reflect it back to people in a way that's hopefully relatable. So I don't think my family minds. I've never done a bit that I wouldn't do to their face."

Rosie's brothers and sisters haven't commented on her remarks. Family friends have said they hope there will be some normal relations between the star and her dad before long, so Rosie's children can bond with their grandpa.

Who knows? Things might change now that Rosie is free of the massive pressures of the daily TV show and the monthly magazine she co-owned in 2001 and 2002. Judging from remarks she's made recently, she doesn't see Edward O'Donnell as all bad anymore. She now sees her dad as one of eight children who was not loved enough.

It's a start.

CHAPTER 8

Rosie was totally happy with and devoted to her son, Parker, as during the second year of "The Rosie O'Donnell Show," she saw its ratings soar skyward. As much as she loved Parker and enjoyed his precocious smarts, she still yearned for a daughter whom she could dress, teach and pamper as the ultimate link to her own dead mother.

There was no man in her life to father a child. Although Rosie was quoted as saying she didn't need a man because Parker and the show were very fulfilling, this wasn't the whole truth. It was a "cover" story encouraged by her publicists, the cautious men and women who advised the star and strained to protect her image.

She believed them when they told her she had to project an image that she was working exhaustively to earn extra income for her boy's education, taking on outside projects in addition to her show and so had no time for a relationship with a man. It was a useful fiction.

To build up a big fat nest egg for the era after the show had run its course, as all talk shows did sooner or later, Rosie endorsed products and shot funny commercials for K-mart and signed a $3 million contract to write a memoir. All this was for Parker — and for the daughter Rosie dreamed about daily.

Not telling the truth about her sexual preference wasn't natural for Rosie O'Donnell, who was admired for her brash outspokenness, but the "suits" talked her into it. And she probably would have stopped short of complete honesty even without their pressure, for although she talked tough, she was somewhat afraid of being up front about this aspect of her life.

While Rosie's image-managers tried to maintain a fictional image of their supposedly man-hungry and lovelorn star, in reality her love life was in turmoil — and there wasn't a man in sight.

After splitting with Michelle Blakely, Rosie found herself drawn to Kate Fitzgerald. Rosie found solace in planning to adopt a second child in the company of Parker's new nanny. Lonely without Michelle, the needy diva began to spend more time with this new woman.

At first, they shared a commitment to the boy's well-being, but soon they were sharing more than that. The nanny, who had acting credits, was in awe of her multitalented employer. Deprived of affection and up-close approval now that her two-year romance with Michelle had ended, Rosie found comfort and reassurance in the attentions of devoted Kate.

"The couple sometimes take Parker to an outdoor cafe near Rosie's luxury Manhattan apartment," revealed a close source. "In the afternoons they go for walks together, and at night they have candlelight dinners at home."

Rosie even admitted to the pal, "Kate is helping me put the pieces of my broken heart back together."

But Rosie soon tired of Kate, and found herself pining for old flame Michelle, who had moved to California to try to resurrect the career she'd given up to stand in Rosie's shadow. Rosie and Michelle had stayed in touch, and Rosie made it clear to Michelle that while she dallied with Kate, she ached to be back with Michelle.

Kate, who shared Rosie's apartment as a live-in nanny, could only watch while Rosie connived with Michelle behind her back. "Rosie is whispering sweet nothings in Michelle's ear," a source confided. "Rosie and Michelle broke up eight months ago, but they never stopped loving each other. Now they're secretly seeing each other behind Kate's back and there's plotting afoot!"

Rosie told a pal at the time: "'Kate's a good person, but she's not really my type. She was there for me when I was getting over Michelle — and she's wonderful with Parker. But we can't stay together.'"

Rosie's best-laid plans, however, came to naught, leaving three people — herself, Michelle and Kate — brokenhearted.

Michelle still cared deeply for Rosie, but she had reluctantly decided she ought to move to Hollywood to start rebuilding her acting career. She had to get work to support herself in her new life without

Rosie. She was surprised and overjoyed when the star telephoned barely two months after they'd parted.

First Rosie told Michelle that she missed her "deeply." When Michelle replied that she felt the same way, the diva said she'd soon be flying west to appear on several television shows. She accepted Michelle's invitation to reunite and stay with her in Beverly Hills.

When Rosie arrived in mid-February, she rented a hotel room, but an insider noted that she spent most nights in Michelle's apartment. A friend of the star reported that Michelle reached out to the woman she still cared for, gave her an apartment key, and even put a car seat in her Mustang convertible for Parker, who was then 20 months old.

The reunion included a tender Valentine's Day, but the couple couldn't solve the problem that had parted them back in Manhattan. Michelle's effort to persuade Rosie that coming out as gay wouldn't destroy her career or economic future — or Parker's future — was no more successful this time.

Once again, Michelle appealed for a marriage of some sort to make their commitment to each other binding, public and unashamed. She also requested the galimony agreement. This time, said a source, she added something else that troubled Rosie acutely.

Michelle had invested a lot of her time and affection in caring for little Parker. She saw herself as having been practically his co-mother, and now she wanted to officially be his parent after the marriage took place. A friend of the two women confided that Rosie's temper flared at the idea of joint motherhood.

"I'm the only mom he's going to have — and that's it," the star snapped.

While Rosie and Michelle both acknowledge that they cared for each other profoundly, they had to face the facts: the two-year relationship could not be salvaged. Rosie and Parker returned East, where the star resumed plans to adopt a second baby.

Besides her own adoptions, few people in the public or the press know just how much time and effort, in addition to financial support, that Rosie has devoted to adoption issues.

She has done outstanding work to help children of all ages.

"Rosie goes far beyond just sending checks or appearing at fund-raising events," one observer said in the third year of her demanding show. "Rosie's a hands-on person in what moves her, and adoption's extremely important to her."

Rosie has had enough therapy to know that she identifies with parentless children. With her beloved mother gone and her dad frustratingly out of reach, she's responded deeply and emotionally to the need these children — like all children — have for nurturing and love in a perfectly ordinary environment.

It became important to Rosie in 1997 that Parker not be a lonely only child. Having grown up with four siblings, Rosie wanted him to have siblings to play with and scrap with and love.

Once again, Rosie applied to adopt an infant.

While she waited, Rosie honed her show and

recharged her batteries on short trips to Florida with Parker. After a few months, there was also a very capable male nanny on duty during these jet jaunts to the Miami Beach area, where close friend Madonna and other celebrity pals had well-protected homes.

That nanny was to come in real handy before too long, because in late 1997, Rosie's family grew with the addition of new baby Chelsea Belle — the girl Rosie had long dreamed of having.

That Rosie was able to adopt her second child only months after beginning the process was a surprise to some, as typical couples often wait up to five years to get a baby. But Rosie refused to apologize for letting her money and celebrity do the talking when it came to adoption.

"It was one time where I was not going to beat myself up over being a celebrity," Rosie admitted. "It's not like I didn't have to go through the process, but to deny that who I am didn't help things along would be a lie. The truth is, having money helps in every situation."

Though many couples have to wait five years or even longer to adopt a baby, Rosie was able to complete the process in little more than a month. "It is not uncommon for celebrities to agree in advance to pay the living and medical expenses for a birth mother, in an effort to ensure that they get a healthy baby," adoption expert Jennifer Potter told the Enquirer at the time of Chelsea's adoption.

"The cost of such an arrangement can go as high as $40,000 to $50,000, compared to standard adoption fees that average $12,000 or less.

It's no more difficult for a popular celebrity to adopt a healthy newborn baby than it is for them to get a good table at a top restaurant!"

Parker loved his new sister . . . sort of. It was a classic situation. Parker wasn't aware that his mother wanted more children. She had said so often and in cheery anticipation, but to media folk and friends, not to Parker.

"Rosie's baby girl looks so much like Parker people are going to take them for true brother and sister," confided a close friend of the family. "But Parker is not quite as happy as Rosie with his look-alike sister. He's been rough with Chelsea whenever he gets the chance. Rosie knows that Parker's behavior is normal for a rambunctious little boy suddenly playing second fiddle to a new sibling. But she said, 'We're going to put a stop to that!'"

Soon enough, however she did it, Rosie managed to get the message across to Parker. In her own way, the celebrity mom was playing her new role perfectly, and the family grew closer together.

CHAPTER 9

As Rosie drove herself more and more in 1997 to keep the laughs and excitement coming on "The Rosie O'Donnell Show," she drove her black Cadillac SUV more and more to the Mickey D's drive-up window. What with the superhuman demands of a daily talk show, offers to do commercials pouring in as the show's ratings skyrocketed, and rumors that Michelle Blakely had returned East to appear in a play and explore a reunion with her, who could blame Rosie if she wanted a large fries with it all?

According to a friend, Rosie slid into the cycle in February when she was doing shows in Los Angeles and tanking up on pizza, pasta and chili dogs. Madonna had urged her in vain to cut back on all that get-fat-fast food and avoid McDonald's.

Her friends' appeals fell on deaf ears, and Rosie's weight rose on a tide of Ring Dings, Ho-Ho's, fried chicken and potatoes, large cartons of Chinese takeout, and any other fattening flotsam.

In mid-1997, she was said to be up to 210 pounds — a bit of a strain for a 5' 7" woman to carry.

"She hits all of her favorite restaurants and stuffs herself silly," confided one concerned friend. "One L.A. greasy spoon — which specializes in chilly dogs — even hung out a banner to welcome her to town! All of Rosie's friends wish they could make her see she's spiraling out of control.

"But she told me, 'Some people smoke and some people drink too much. I eat. Everyone's got a crutch. All I know is I'm miserable when I'm thinner. I want to enjoy life — and I'm doing it. Is that such a big crime?'"

It's not like the big-boned woman from Commack hasn't tried. She made a genuine effort. A compassionate person who realized that many people in her national audience struggled with the same problem, she thought carefully about how she might help them and herself. Then she presented her weight control plan on television.

She was starting a club for anyone who wanted to join her in a program of sensible eating and exercise to lose the pounds. Friends of the star were impressed, since she'd shown little enthusiasm for any sport or exercise since she graduated from high school. There were physical activities she enjoyed. Riding motorcycles or Jet Skis were two at which she excelled, but her past record with exercise regimes had not been good.

"I wasn't really heavy until I was older," Rosie said at the time. "I was on every sports team. I was the senior class president. I was very popular in high school. It wasn't until I became an adult and wasn't doing as

A rare photo of young Rosie with her mom, Roseann. Rosie was only 10 when her mother died of cancer

Rosie's Commack South High School yearbook photo. Even then, she was an overachiever

At 17, Rosie was fit and athletic

The drama queen – Rosie plays a fairy in a high school production

*Rosie invited the best-looking guy in her high school to the prom.
"It was a friendly thing, not physical," said the date*

*Rosie's father Edward, dubbed "The Head of The Irish Drinking
People," by his daughter on national television*

Rosie won critical praise for her role as a dental hygienist in the sitcom "Gimme a Break" with Nell Carter (rear left) in 1986

Performing stand-up comedy, Rosie once won the "Star Search" competition five times

An up-and-coming Rosie is ready to take on the world

*Fast friends Rosie and Madonna shared a common bond
– both had lost their mothers at an early age*

Rosie (left) in "A League of Their Own"

The comedienne appeared with Emilio Estevez and Richard Dreyfuss in "Another Stakeout"

Rosie played Meg Ryan's best friend in "Sleepless in Seattle"

Still promoting a glamorous front, a made-up Rosie appears at an awards ceremony (above). The star brought her pet dog as a date (right) to the premiere of "Exit to Eden"

In "The Flintstones," Rick Moranis and Rosie played Barney and Betty Rubble

Weighing in at a svelte 150, Rosie played an S&M dominatrix in "Exit to Eden" with Dan Aykroyd. Upon seeing herself in the film years later, she said, "I had an anxiety attack"

While promoting one image on her talk show, Rosie steered an alternative path with girlfriend Michelle Blakely in 1995 (above). Rosie swings a bat for charity (left)

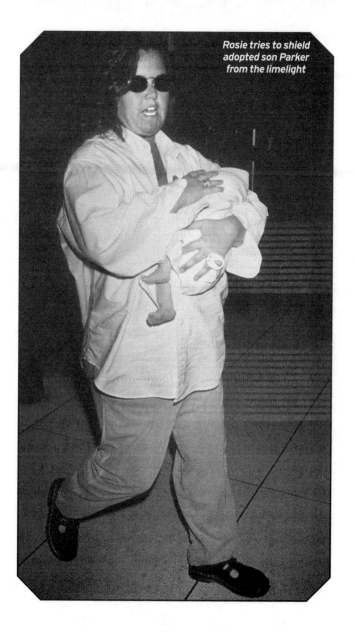

Rosie tries to shield adopted son Parker from the limelight

Rosie with David Johansen in "Car 54, Where Are You?" (above) and in popular kid flick "Harriet the Spy" (right)

Rosie starred with good friend Rita Wilson and Demi Moore in "Now and Then"

Rosie with her "dream guy" Tom Cruise (above), and sporting his name above her heart (below)

Two moms and a baby: Rosie and former live-in love Michelle Blakely take a stroll with Parker in Manhattan. The happy couple enjoy some personal time in Miami (far right). Rosie and Michelle eventually broke up when Rosie refused to marry her

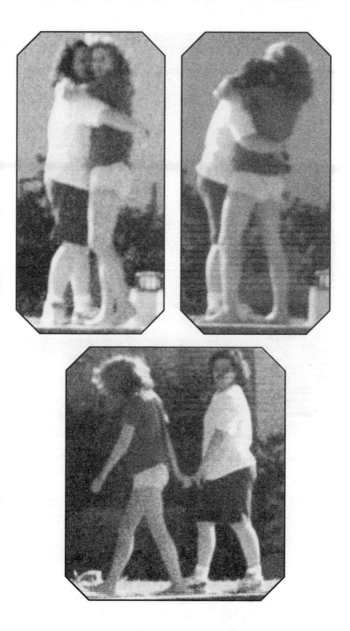

A tearful Rosie accepts an Emmy in 1997

*"The Queen of Nice" image worked so well that
Rosie was cast as a nun in 1998's "Wide Awake"*

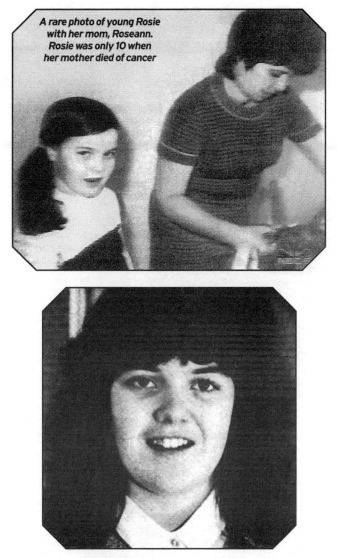

A rare photo of young Rosie with her mom, Roseann. Rosie was only 10 when her mother died of cancer

Rosie's Commack South High School yearbook photo. Even then, she was an overachiever

At 17, Rosie was fit and athletic

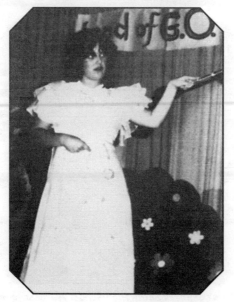

The drama queen - Rosie plays a fairy in a high school production

Rosie invited the best-looking guy in her high school to the prom. "It was a friendly thing, not physical," said the date

Rosie's father Edward, dubbed "The Head of The Irish Drinking People," by his daughter on national television

Rosie won critical praise for her role as a dental hygienist in the sitcom "Gimme a Break" with Nell Carter (rear left) in 1986

Performing stand-up comedy, Rosie once won the "Star Search" competition five times

An up-and-coming Rosie is ready to take on the world

Fast friends Rosie and Madonna shared a common bond – both had lost their mothers at an early age

Rosie (left) in "A League of Their Own"

The comedienne appeared with Emilio Estevez and Richard Dreyfuss in "Another Stakeout"

Rosie played Meg Ryan's best friend in "Sleepless in Seattle"

Still promoting a glamorous front, a made-up Rosie appears at an awards ceremony (above). The star brought her pet dog as a date (right) to the premiere of "Exit to Eden"

In "The Flintstones," Rick Moranis and Rosie played Barney and Betty Rubble

Weighing in at a svelte 150, Rosie played an S&M dominatrix in "Exit to Eden" with Dan Aykroyd. Upon seeing herself in the film years later, she said, "I had an anxiety attack"

While promoting one image on her talk show, Rosie steered an alternative path with girlfriend Michelle Blakely in 1995 (above). Rosie swings a bat for charity (left)

Rosie tries to shield adopted son Parker from the limelight

Rosie with David Johansen in "Car 54, Where Are You?" (above) and in popular kid flick "Harriet the Spy" (right)

Rosie starred with good friend Rita Wilson and Demi Moore in "Now and Then"

Rosie with her "dream guy" Tom Cruise (above), and sporting his name above her heart (below)

Two moms and a baby: Rosie and former live-in love Michelle Blakely take a stroll with Parker in Manhattan. The happy couple enjoy some personal time in Miami (far right). Rosie and Michelle eventually broke up when Rosie refused to marry her

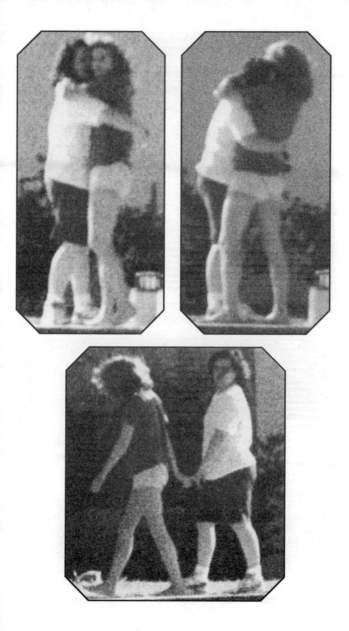

A tearful Rosie accepts an Emmy in 1997

"The Queen of Nice" image worked so well that Rosie was cast as a nun in 1998's "Wide Awake"

many sports that my weight became more of an issue."

She admits that she hates her body. What's more, Rosie confesses, she always has. She doesn't even look in mirrors. She's so distressed by her own appearance that she tries never to be naked. In fact, if she could have sex with her clothes on, she would.

"I am the dieting queen," she wrote in 2002, "but along with the other four billion diet queens in this country, I never stick with the program."

What's more, she doesn't even know when she's seriously overweight. "At 230, I become invisible to myself. I need other peoples' eyes," she admits. She wonders why nobody's told her how bloated she is.

Ruefully she recalls dating a woman years ago who was starving herself to be thin. Rosie agreed to work out with her twice a day at a gym and eat a low-calorie "healthy" diet. Being a "little crazy with love," Rosie hardly noticed the pounds go, since she was too concerned with reassuring her anorexic friend that she, too, was talented and worthy.

It was another case of Rosie not looking at Rosie.

When, to her surprise, she received an invitation to the wedding of Donald and Marla Trump, she faced a fashion crisis: all her closet offered was "sweatpants and biker shorts." What would she wear? A kind friend guided Rosie to a hip clothing store, where she got an even bigger surprise. She fit into a glamorous size 10 Armani suit. She bought three of them.

Rosie hadn't been a size 10 "since the eighth grade." It shook her so much that she made a beeline from the sleek store to a Baskin-Robbins, where she wolfed down a waffle cone with two scoops of chocolate chip ice cream.

Why did she jump off the wagon when she was a good-looking size 10? Tell-it-like-it-is Rosie O'Donnell admits in "Find Me" that she missed her old body, the same one she loathed in the mirror.

"Fat is a protector," she diagnosed. "I didn't like being thin. I felt like people could come too close. After my brief relationship fizzled, so did my trips to the gym."

She could put on her armor of fat again. The threat of intimacy had almost menaced her when she was 29 and in love with a sweet, kind and handsome man. Proposing marriage, he assured her that the size of her body didn't matter. Caught in her mixed feelings that marriage to him might be both thrilling and "repulsive," she couldn't believe her girth wouldn't repel him.

Unconsciously, she moved to make certain that it did. As they grew closer over the months, she piled on more weight. Each additional pound moved her one step away from him. She ended the romance by "using flesh for padding. I bubble-wrapped my heart."

Rosie doesn't pretend her fear of being trim makes sense to other people not carrying her emotional baggage. Her weight is only an external sign of what makes Rosie O'Donnell tell the world in the plainest language and without pride that she is difficult to love. Add to this her blunt manner and the fact that she often doesn't — or doesn't know how to — explain her abruptly changeable behavior.

In April 1997, Rosie was so popular and admired that she received the queen-sized compliment of being invited to host the annual dinner and gala of the White House Correspondents Association. That was practically on par with the Oscars, a real feather in her cap.

She never went to the dinner. A few weeks before the gala, first lady Hillary Clinton showed up on Rosie's television show as a gesture of good will, and from what she said it was clear she was looking forward to a friendly fun-packed dinner. By tradition these galas were stylish affairs of sophistication and bipartisan humor.

Everyone working on preparations for the special celebration, which raised money for a worthy cause, was startled when Rosie O'Donnell abruptly canceled.

Her sole explanation: "personal reasons."

Many in the tight world of Washington power and egos saw Rosie's behavior as disrespectful to both the spoiled and sensitive capital press corps and to the White House. Some shrewd folks down in the District of Columbia wondered what gesture of conciliation might come from the savvy public relations firm guiding and protecting the show and the star.

After many months, their attention was diverted by a stream of new Rosie developments. Rosie and the White House both seemed willing to let bygones be bygones. While Jay Leno, David Letterman, and other comedians took aim at both President Clinton and his administration, Rosie was not among the most active spear throwers.

At the time, the television talk-show host had other things and people on her mind. For years, she'd shown great admiration for Tom Cruise, openly voicing her intense desire to get the handsome movie star as a guest. Viewers unaware of Rosie's sexual identity assumed that she had a crush on him, and she didn't discourage this misconception. She really liked him, his rugged good looks, and his work as an actor. Having him appear on her show would be like having David Cassidy come down off the wall in her bedroom back in Commack.

The thought of the plump diva possibly cuddling up with hunk Cruise delighted her warmhearted fans, and this public approval was also good for her image. Rosie's heart was in it, too, in a manner of speaking. Knowing she would probably meet him at Hollywood's glamorous, star-studded Moving Picture Ball, Rosie showed up at the schmoozefest in a dress with a plunging neckline that showed his name written as a fake tattoo on her chest, just above her heart.

The stunt succeeded, certainly with the photographers covering the event. Cruise good-naturedly kissed her — more than once — so there'd be plenty of pictures to please editors, press agents and not-very-romantic producers working with the two hot celebrities.

More than a year passed before Cruise finally was able to appear on Rosie's show. It was well worth the anticipation. She was delighted, her audience was thrilled, and her ratings spiked.

Rosie's other most desired "get," in the jargon of the talk-show business, was a superstar she had dreamed about since she was nine. It was a singer-actress-director-producer who almost never went on talk shows. When world-class talent Barbra

Streisand finally came to the show, it was superdiva versus superdiva. Streisand is an adored and revered doyenne of the music and film industries, and an even bigger control freak than O'Donnell.

Streisand had her own exact ideas about makeup, lighting, and everything except the temperature in the studio. Rosie didn't put up a fuss about any of her idol's demands. Rosie was loving life with son Parker and daughter Chelsea, and she was ready to do almost anything to have her long-anticipated Streisand experience.

Difficult perfectionists though they are, both entertainers were also total professionals. Neither was foolish enough to mess up a coast-to-coast show. Rosie's dream had come true. She knew that her beloved mother, who was such a Streisand fan, would have loved it.

Then there's the acclaimed and lovely young actress Angelina Jolie. Rosie has mentioned her tenderly on the show and written that she's had several dreams about the slim, pretty Angelina, who doesn't hide the fact that she's a bit of a nonconformist herself. Angelina's been open about her appetite for life, her passionate nature, and her tattoos.

Rosie's never elaborated on exactly what took place in her dreams of the sexy and vivacious Ms. Jolie. Maybe in Rosie's nocturnal fantasy world the two of them showed each other their tattoos?

Rosie has made seven trips to tattoo parlors, and the skin art permanently adorns her flesh. When she was young, she imagined a picture of what bad guys looked like: dirty hair, black T-shirts and tattoos were standard features of people to avoid, she told herself.

Over time and trouble, a lonely young Rosie changed. She wasn't satisfied with her life, and began to think about how to make changes. She came to conclude that a tattoo was more than ink and would in some mystical way "mark a transition from one mind-set to another."

Scared, weak, and worried in ways she couldn't put into words, Rosie gathered her emotional strength for an escape from the "dark ugliness" of her daily being, she has said. She was sure there was something better. It was hard to explain this discontent to other people, but Rosie was sure she was right. She was announcing a new Rosie, even if she wasn't entirely sure who that was yet. When she found a tattoo parlor in a run-down storefront, she went in and was greeted by "a burly biker man" who was friendly and smiling.

Unlike other adult males she knew, he wasn't self-centered or intimidating. He said he'd draw whatever she wanted, and didn't press her.

Rosie chose a cross with a rose and a heart from the many patterns displayed. Uncertain about whether she was really brave enough to have it where many people might notice it, she asked him to "do" it on the inside of her right ankle.

One hour and $80 later, the new, free and tattooed Rosie O'Donnell left the shop, convinced that she had left behind her old identity and the old body that had somehow "betrayed" her. If the notion seems puzzling, it does fit into her long-standing and publicly declared hatred of her own body.

Since it is so hard for Rosie and other women to

meet society's unreal standards for physical attractiveness, Rosie has chosen defiance. If she doesn't try to meet society's standards, she can't end up a loser. She can't be defeated if she won't play their game. She's long felt that she is an outsider, and with this self-perception she can beat the sense of inferiority and inadequacy that our media-driven culture imposes on so many women.

Over the six years of her show, she made several efforts to present support systems for ongoing weight loss, and she addressed the deep issues of perfection in therapy. She's struggled to find a way to feel right about herself exactly as she is. Doing this with candor and good humor, Rosie has displayed a big-boned humanity that shows people that self-control is worthwhile, but perfection isn't necessary.

As the popularity of "The Rosie O'Donnell Show" soared and raked in millions for her and the syndication company, Rosie showed in dozens of ways her growing belief in her own worth and wisdom. Her early fear that North American audiences would abandon an "outsider" — based on the cautious advice of the conservative suits at the syndication corporation and well-meaning public relations "experts" — slowly began to fade.

The tattoos kept coming. A thin band of roses, a full bouquet of flowers, and others. Through all the ups and downs, they didn't fade.

CHAPTER 10

IT WAS IN THE APRIL 21, 1997 EDITION OF "TIME" MAGAZINE THAT ROSIE O'DONNELL, "CHEERLEADER," WAS NAMED ONE OF THE MAGAZINE'S 25 MOST INFLUENTIAL AMERICANS.

"Yes, there are loftier, more laudable show-business goals than becoming the Merv Griffin of one's generation, but thankfully Rosie O'Donnell, 35, was not consumed by more grandiose dreams," read the printed accolade. "As a TV addict growing up in Commack, New York, she fell in love with the ingratiating style of talk-show hosts like Griffin and Mike Douglas."

"I tried to make a show that an eight-year-old kid could watch with his mother and grandma that would entertain everyone," said O'Donnell.

"Since its debut last summer," the "Time" piece continued, "The Rosie O'Donnell Show, broadcast all over the country and contracted to run at least until the year 2001, has become the second-highest-rated daytime talk show on TV behind Oprah's. In Los Angeles, Rosie has even been known to beat the grande dame . . . If Rosie has a formula it is "Love thy neighbor to the right.'"

Meanwhile, the real Rosie was showing another side of the Queen of Nice.

At one big showbiz event, Rosie cussed out a photographer who a few weeks earlier had rudely pushed a friend of hers aside so he could snap a salable picture of some star. Rosie read him the riot act as other celebrities gaped. They didn't have the nerve to do that — photographers and journalists were dangerous to tangle with any time.

Then came the already mentioned first round in her knockdown-dragout fight with acid-tongued Joan Rivers, who'd ridiculed Rosie's pal Janeane Garofalo for being underdressed at a formal event. This was to escalate into television's version of the Hundred Years War.

"She totally made fun of me," Garofalo declared on Rosie's show. "She was like, outrageous about what I wore."

"I don't like that kind of comedy," Rosie declared. "I always had a problem when Joan Rivers did it. It's not funny to make fun of somebody's weight or especially of some of the public figures that were struggling and in detox centers."

Then Rosie brought up an especially sore subject — the tragic 1987 suicide of Joan's beloved husband Edgar Rosenberg.

"I thought that people's jokes about her husband's death would have changed her," Rosie said.

Joan, in turn, shot back on her syndicated radio

show, saying she was hurt by the public attack.

Rosie, unconcerned, confided to a friend that the feud was, at the very least, good for ratings and she didn't mind talking about Joan because she thought the performer was over the hill.

The rancor coming from the Queen of Nice raised a lot of eyebrows. But should people have really been surprised? The moniker had been imposed on Rosie by a journalist who didn't know her as well as her legion of friends. Rosie isn't a fundamentally mean person, but she has never been wholly comfortable with the "nice" designation, and she's talked about this honestly for more than five years.

"I'm not really that nice. I'm a normal person," Rosie declared as far back as 1998. "'Nice' to me has a connotation of passivity. I'm not passive."

Whitney Houston would certainly agree. She provoked Rosie's ire when she canceled a scheduled appearance on "The Rosie O'Donnell Show" — sent word that she was sick — and then appeared that evening with her notorious husband, Bobby Brown, on the David Letterman show. Houston must have thought that Rosie called it a night early.

Rosie felt she'd been publicly humiliated in front of millions. Everyone in TV expected her to retaliate, and she didn't disappoint.

When she learned of Rosie's righteous rage, Houston optimistically tried to put out the fire by sending over an extraordinarily large bouquet of the finest flowers. It must have cost hundreds of dollars. It was money wasted.

When word got back to Whitney that Rosie was still angry, somebody cleverly advised Houston to send a grander and more expensive expression of atonement. Figuring that Rosie was a huge softie about her infant daughter, Chelsea, they sent a $10,000 antique rocking horse.

Chelsea, like brother Parker, already had a mountain of toys and other fine items bought by Rosie and pals like Madonna. More important, Rosie's sense of being disrespected was not abated. It took her two seconds to decide to send the rocking horse to a children's hospital.

She sent a blunt message back to Houston. The only way you might possibly make up for your awful sin would be to show some class and come do the show as promised.

Whitney Houston is a big talent and an intelligent woman, but she wasn't willing to run the risk of facing Rosie in front of a national audience of O'Donnell fans.

Lucky for her, Rosie soon had something else on her mind.

Rosie was in a new, intense love relationship. She wasn't trying to hide it, but it was more than 10 weeks before it showed up on the media's radar screen. Kate Fitzgerald was gone, replaced by a male nanny who did his job well without any complications.

Rosie had been making her usual round of benefits and fund-raisers for all the causes she thought worthwhile. In December of 1997, she was at an event where her older brother, Danny, a respected lawyer, was also present. Midway through the evening, Rosie later told close friends, Danny walked up to her and casually told her that he'd just met a woman whom Rosie might like to know. They were talking together minutes later.

The "together" was to last. The pretty woman with short blonde hair was Kelli Carpenter, a marketing executive with Nickelodeon. She was bright, warm, and plainly attracted to O'Donnell. Five years younger than the lonely, bighearted star, she had a personality that suited Rosie's, and she liked kids.

Old flames Michelle Blakely and Kate Fitzgerald were devastated. Rosie and Michelle's doomed, on-again off-again relationship had been 'on' shortly before Rosie met Kelli — but in January 1998, Rosie broke the news to Michelle that she'd met someone new.

According to a source, Rosie told Michelle: " 'She's perfect for me. I'm sorry about us. It wasn't meant to be.' "

By February 1998, the connection between the two women was so strong that they went to the elegant Cartier jewelry shop on Fifth Avenue to buy special rings for each other, a close friend revealed.

"It's exactly like we're engaged," Kelli reportedly enthused. The ring Rosie gave her new love was "breathtaking — two bands of platinum encrusted with diamonds." Kelli reciprocated with a fine gold band that said she shared the commitment.

Rosie-watchers confirm that Kelli began spending a lot of time at the star's midtown Manhattan apartment. It wasn't long before Carpenter took the next step and introduced Rosie to her parents. The star and the TV executive became nearly inseparable right after that. No one else can say exactly what the two hoped for, but they were united in facing the future. Whether they ever anticipated that Kelli would give birth to Vivienne Rose O'Donnell four and a half years later remains their family secret.

When her favorite star headed west to tape some episodes of her show in Los Angeles, Kelli right away took a few days off from work to fly out to join Rosie in a spectacular rented Beverly Hills mansion.

The following month, Rosie gave a pair of sold-out performances one weekend at Caesar's Palace in Las Vegas while Kelli, Parker and Chelsea lived it up with her in a four-bedroom suite at the hotel. Rosie was thrilled to hear that the sky-high suite had once housed another influential American, the great Elvis Presley.

"I swear to God," the TV funnylady jokingly confided to a friend, "The King's apparition appeared and told me and Kelli, 'I don't care what people say, there's nothing wrong with two people who love each other being together. Keep the faith.' Then Elvis disappeared."

Rosie added with a chuckle, "Now that I know Elvis approves, I have no doubt that Kelli and I are meant for each other."

Real-life observers in Las Vegas said Rosie made no secret of her conviction she and Kelli were "meant for each other." Then they were back to Los Angeles for a Cedars-Sinai Medical Center fund-raiser, where Rosie was honored as a "Woman of Courage." Her love was at her side, beaming.

The no-longer-lonely diva was still eating at full speed, and on this visit to the City of Angels, she introduced her dear companion to one of her favorite restaurants, the popular Chin Chin. The calories flowed like an avalanche in a dim sum "feast" that an observer called "huge," and the compulsive eater topped it off by scarfing no fewer than 15 of their chocolate-dipped gourmet fortune cookies. A record for the Chin Chin, but Rosie had an excellent reason for setting it.

"I'm not stopping until I find a fortune that I like," she told amazed onlookers proudly.

That's what a "Star Wars" fan might call Rosie's "prime directive." She hasn't needed any Federation of Planets to set her basic principle. She's an extremely strong-willed person who isn't embarrassed anymore to do things her own way.

By the middle of the rambunctious six-year party that was "The Rosie O'Donnell Show," the star was starting to speak out and be herself more and more. This was slowly but surely becoming clearer to everyone. Some of the public and a few of the sharp-tongued media people were beginning to get the message.

CHAPTER 11

THE QUEEN OF NICE BEGAN TO SHOCK EVEN SOME OF HER MOST LOYAL FANS AS SHE TACKLED ISSUES LARGE AND SMALL, INCREASINGLY USING HER SHOW AS A SOAPBOX TO PUSH FOR GUN CONTROL, TO TALK ABOUT GOD, AND EVEN TO BLAST A POPULAR PURPLE DINOSAUR NAMED BARNEY.

Rosie O'Donnell was probably the only talk-show host on North American television who went to the movie theater to see "lovable" Barney on the big screen and hated it.

The kids she took to the movie, including son Parker, nieces and nephews, thought it was just wonderful, and millions of children and adults agreed.

But the day after seeing the movie, Rosie floored viewers of all ages, declaring that Barney was "the worst movie ever made, pure torture . . . I would rather have a root canal."

She didn't mind Barney on the small screen at home, she said, because she could leave the room.

Some critics of her unusual assault have wondered whether her condemnation reflected her loyalty to Barney's competition, Sesame Street, on which she had frequently appeared.

Having a strong opinion on everything is pure Rosie, and her friends say that's not likely to change. Sometimes, under firm pressure from people who she realizes love her, she has the flexibility to adjust . . . maybe a little bit . . . at least on a trial basis.

Her ever-present weight problem was one area her close friends felt they had to try to pressure her. Maybe she didn't see herself, but they saw her. As she continued to eat worse than a gorilla, her weight reached 215 pounds in spring 1998, and Rosie got a talking-to by two of those near and dear to her. It was getting dangerous. Madonna and Kelli put it simply: time to tone up and slim down. For starters, lose 15 pounds — and lose them soon.

For Rosie the new effort included yoga, as Madonna suggested, plus a half hour daily on an exercise bike and a diet of energy-boosting dishes perfected by a nutritionist. There were also sessions with a therapist that featured "visualizing" being thinner.

Maybe this time it would work, since the star wouldn't have to face the tough challenge alone. Kelli, so close and caring, promised she'd be Rosie's trainer and help her stick to the program.

Rosie began the yoga, and started to work out on the bike.

If she didn't get too far, many fans would say that wasn't a bad thing.

As part of living a healthier lifestyle, Rosie bought

a Victorian mansion, up the Hudson River in Nyack, N.Y., so she, Kelli, Parker and Chelsea could head north every weekend to quieter and safer country living. In the sophisticated town of Nyack, where many writers and stage celebrities had homes, she paid $770,000 for the mansion that had long been the residence of Broadway star Helen Hayes, who christened it Pretty Penny (it cost one), and screenwriter Charles MacArthur. The place had 22 rooms, six fireplaces, a wine cellar, a pool, beautiful view, lovely grounds — and supposedly a ghost, the spirit of Hayes's 19-year-old daughter, who had died of polio.

Rosie didn't rule out the supernatural — in fact, she was drawn to it. After reading a book about encounters with aliens called "Confirmation," Rosie invited the book's author, Whitley Strieber, on her show to talk about the possibility that aliens exist and have been in contact with select citizens of earth — maybe even Rosie herself!

Strieber disclosed that Rosie believed that aliens were secretly here on Earth, visiting from other planets and having close encounters with humans.

Commenting on his written reports that space travelers were here, hiding implants in humans, Rosie turned to her studio audience during a commercial break and, touching a spot by her right ear, confided, "I really think I could have one of those implants." She'd spoken on camera in earlier broadcasts about accepting the notion that aliens had come to Earth. Many other people — some major stars — have long been convinced of this.

But it came as a shock for the usually very down-to-earth Rosie to suddenly start waxing on about alien encounters. Rosie herself told the Enquirer at the time: "Extraterrestrial life is something we should all be curious about."

Strieber added that "Rosie told me she believes space aliens are real. And she believes our experiences with aliens are something that should be taken seriously. A celebrity of Rosie's stature willing to declare herself on behalf of the close encounter witness is just wonderful."

There were other questions that Rosie sought to have answered — such as whether we can communicate with the dead.

A therapist had earlier tried to help Rosie deal with the fear of being abandoned, which stemmed from her mother's death and inhibited her from developing relationships at the time. Friends urged her next to speak with medium and author George Anderson, who had a remarkable reputation for being able to channel the deceased to their living loved ones.

Anderson paid a personal visit to Rosie's Manhattan home, and impressed Rosie by reeling off the song the elder Roseann O'Donnell would sing to Rosie and her sister, plus the names of aunts and uncles who had passed on. Anderson also conveyed a message to Rosie from her long-dead mom during his visit.

"My mother said I shouldn't be so pissed off all the time," Rosie said. "It's like a great weight was lifted off my shoulders. It was very touching, it really was."

Rosie made up her mind to try to let go of the rage she knew was hurting her. But that was easier said than done.

By the spring of 1999, Rosie was living through a private and public hell that left her in painful crying jags, and even led her to confess to her TV audience: "I'm a wreck. I really think I need some medication. I have such a high stress level."

Several high-profile incidents sparked her breakdown.

First, Broadway star Audra McDonald fainted during a Drama League tribute to Rosie. Though McDonald was OK, "I was a weeping ball of nothing," Rosie confessed to her viewers. "I was hysterical — crying for the rest of the show. I was lost for the rest of the night. I'm hysterical — crying during the Fosse number. When I went up to give my speech, I was crying again. When I got home, I'm still crying and I call Audra like five times."

Rosie was also stressed out from the burdens of keeping her show at the top of the ratings heap, as well as her charitable work with the Make-A-Wish and All For Kids Foundations.

"If Rosie wasn't so bighearted, she wouldn't be such a wreck," said a friend. "If she would just say 'no,' the pressure would ease."

To make matters worse, Rosie was roasted in the press after a high school band from Atlanta raised $81,000 to travel to New York to be on Rosie's show — without being invited!

"The show never told the band they could appear," a show insider said. "The band has 128 members and the stage just isn't big enough. But the band came anyway."

Rosie tried to tell her side of the story, but it was a

public relations disaster. "Even the mayor of New York got in on the act by meeting and greeting the band at a local restaurant," a source said. "Rosie told me, 'I've been burning the candle at both ends with my kids and the show and the charities — but the brouhaha with the band crushed me. It was a kick in the teeth.'"

Seeking some sort of solace and comfort during this troubled time, Rosie found herself drawn to a stronger belief in God.

"It's the way to go," she said at the time. "I'm all for that God thing. I'm big on that now. It's my new thing. Whatever your God is — Jewish, Muslim, Buddha — I don't care. Whatever you think God is, you have to get in touch with that. Let's get the God thing going around. Get it going."

Rosie had been a practicing Catholic until her mother's death. She angrily withdrew from God, whom she blamed for taking away her beloved, vivacious mother.

In an emotional moment on her show, Rosie told the audience: "I'm praying for healing lately for everyone, starting with me — that I'm not so full of angst about everything. Praying for my own healing. Praying for everyone's healing."

She seemed finally to have found some peace in her return to religion, but the controversies continued to pile up.

Children were Rosie's constant concern and, for some time, she'd been horrified following news stories of innocent youngsters being shot and killed in the United States. Several high-profile, senseless deaths in mid-1999 culminating with the massacre of students at Columbine High School brought Rosie's anger to a boil.

On her well-remembered show of May 18th — less than a month after the Columbine shootings — Rosie O'Donnell went ballistic on guns. She lashed out against her guest, former "Magnum, P.I." star Tom Selleck, who didn't share her views on abolishing access to guns. Their furious disagreement was so bitter that it was called "one of the most shocking confrontations ever seen on TV."

In a fight that continued for days on camera and in print, people rushed in from all sides to support or denounce Rosie's view that there needs to be more gun control in this country. Most prominent among her opponents in this dispute was Charlton Heston, a senior film star and dedicated president of the influential National Rifle Association.

"This is an obviously angry lady," Heston said, "and it's hard to reason well when you're angry . . . she should be a little less shrill."

Rosie bit her tongue until Heston went after her idol Barbra Streisand.

The very liberal Streisand had produced a movie called "The Long Island Incident," about a woman who was elected to Congress on a gun-control platform after her husband was gunned down in 1993. Heston blasted the film and Streisand in a series of ads and a press conference, calling the diva "the Hanoi Jane of the Second Amendment."

Rosie used her own soapbox to let Heston have it.

"A lot of people are afraid of Charlton Heston — not me!" Rosie thundered on her show. "Listen, Chuck — I know you played Moses, I know you're a big guy in the NRA. Say one more thing about my friend Barbra, I'm gonna kick your butt! You have your beliefs, others have theirs. Leave her alone."

But some viewers were outraged by Rosie's call for change in America's gun laws, claiming that she was a hypocrite. She was happy to take piles of money to do K-mart commercials, they charged, but how could she justify it when K-mart sold guns?

The reply was swift. K-Mart hadn't sold handguns for over 20 years, Rosie shot back. And it had never dealt in assault rifles. With some 4,000 children killed every year by guns, Rosie insisted, it was time to make sure only "responsible" people could get guns. Her allies added a chilling statistic: In the most recent year for which data was available, the number of deaths by handguns in the United States was almost nine times more than the totals for Canada, Britain and Japan combined.

In fact, there was another, secret reason behind Rosie's anti-gun tirade and Rosie's own burgeoning activism against weapons. Watching a late-night TV show one night in 1996 when little Parker was sick, Rosie was shocked to see a report on a 10-year-old boy who had accidentally shot his best pal and killed him.

"When Rosie saw the news report, she was devastated, it changed her life," a source said. "Rosie told me, 'How can any mother go on after their child is killed? I just couldn't bear it. I looked down at little Parker and thought to myself, 'I can do something to help save the lives of children.'

"And that's when Rosie got involved in supporting gun control. She got involved for kids everywhere and for little Parker."

The unsuspecting Selleck wound up in the crosshairs of Rosie's passionate temper — but it was Rosie herself who was soon to get the scare of her life.

A threat had been made against Parker's life by a possible mental case who called Howard Stern's live radio show, broadcast from New York. It was the dreary routine of most callers to the program to imitate Stern's sexually graphic language. Some of the depraved callers went further.

One night, an anonymous phone freak ranting with Stern on the air suddenly threatened to kidnap Rosie O'Donnell's son. The stranger was probably just desperate for attention. However, neither Stern nor Rosie could know that.

Rosie was frightened. She knew that many famous people were menaced by repeated letters or calls from "fans" who fantasized about them incessantly. The phone threat jolted her.

"Rosie's terrified," confided a source close to the star. "She's careful not to act afraid in front of Parker, but this is tearing her apart."

"I was in the studio doing my own show when I was told about the threat," Rosie told the source. "I went right to Parker and held him. I felt helpless, afraid and very angry. I decided it was time to get away from the public. In fact, that's what I'm going to do all summer now that the show's finished for the season. I know the police are trying to find this guy. But for a while I need to go away and just be Mom."

CHAPTER 12

Rosie was pure mother now, a lioness protecting her cubs. She found herself so uneasy she started thinking about selling the mansion in Nyack, where the walls and fences were modest, and buying a residence in Connecticut with more security. In October 1999, she put the Nyack place on the market for $2,750,000.

The family still had their little estate on Star Island in Florida and the huge apartment in Manhattan, so Rosie could take her time looking for the just-right third residence that would be near New York City and yet very secure.

For some reassurance about her own safety, she bought an expensive guard dog. This well-trained German shepherd was supposed to protect her in the broadcast studio and at her country place. Like so many things in Rosie's extraordinary life, this didn't work out exactly as planned. The animal wasn't that good at protection, but it seemed to have a tendency to bite guests on the show. And, Rosie shared with her viewers, the dog also had a gift for peeing behind her couch.

Besides the guard dog, Rosie also sought to protect her children in other ways — as in making sure she'd be around long enough to raise them. She'd privately agonized over her weight for years, but in 1999 she finally did something big about it.

Wanting to set a goal of losing weight and stay with it this time, she decided to go public and set up a support group for herself and millions of her viewers and fans. Launched in January 1999, Rosie called her weight-loss plan the Chubb Club. She'd try to make it fun with a club T-shirt and slogans galore. She had no illusion that it would be easy.

She weighed 208 at the time she began the club — but for the first six months, the club turned out to be a flub, at least for Rosie. In fact, by June, she had gained eight pounds.

But Rosie, for once, didn't abandon the plan entirely. She spent the last half of 1999 adhering to the Chubb Club plan. A whopping 216 pounds in June of that year, Rosie finally buckled down and lost 32 pounds in the next six months.

"What I've been doing since June is simply sticking to the original Chubb Club plan — eating less and moving more!" she said in early 2000. "I realized I needed to introduce some discipline into the more or less haphazard way I was eating. I also eat less sweets than I used to, and I rarely snack."

Losing so much weight was an amazing accomplishment for a woman with so many issues behind her weight. She looked better, felt better and, though she was to pack the pounds back on with a vengeance, for a time she was an inspiration to the millions of women who looked to her as a role model.

Rosie also explained for the first time why she could never risk becoming pregnant. Her family history was too dangerous, she said candidly. The history of alcoholism and cancer frightened her too much. She couldn't take the awful chance of passing either affliction on to a baby.

That didn't mean she couldn't explore even more ways to add to her family. Rosie announced that her plans for children went beyond adoption. She was in the process of becoming qualified as a foster mother under the laws and rules of Florida, where she had a home.

"I went through 30 hours of training on the needs of foster kids, how to help them, what to do and not to do," she reported for the first time. "Teachers and counselors also came to my house. They gave me psychological and emotional tests to make sure I was someone who could do this."

Rosie met all the requirements for certification. Being a foster parent is generally the first step toward possibly adopting a child in most states. She had learned a great deal in raising the two children she'd adopted as infants. She was ready to move to the next level by "making things better for kids" her primary "goal in life now."

Rosie said that women who were pregnant or

had just had a baby now approached her to adopt their babies because they knew she was a wealthy and loving person who could give the infant a better life. In one case, Rosie gave the woman the name of an excellent adoption agency likely to find the baby very good parents. That was easy for the star to do because she'd learned so much about adoption and the agencies, government services, and rules.

The caring star said frankly that she thought she could mother five children. She'd grown up as one of five, so it was feasible and the number had some emotional appeal to her. She was certain from her practical experience that there were all kinds of families — that it didn't matter whether a family was made through adoption, through a combination of fostering and adoption, or through natural childbirth.

She insisted, "All children are from God. All that matters is that children are loved and nourished, and they love back. It's amazing."

The nursery that Warner's built at her studio allowed her to be with Parker and Chelsea for many hours more than other TV performers could spend with their children, the diva observed. Her financial situation let her pay two part-time nannies and other help, she added without a hint of boasting.

Rosie never forgot how she grew up in a family with a modest income, and she's taken great care to try to make sure her children don't become spoiled rich kids. She's aware that she and her children and now Kelli live the life of the wealthy, but the star keeps making efforts to ensure her children remain "regular" and without pretensions.

It hasn't been easy.

The reality is that they live in a world of ease, options, and material comfort afforded by an income of many millions. The high life of the rich and famous comes with its own particular problems, but children may not think about them.

One afternoon when Parker came home from school with several first-grade classmates, she tensed as she heard him speak casually of weekend plans.

"We're flying down to our Florida place in a private jet," her son mentioned matter-of-factly. "My bodyguard's coming with us."

"Why did you say that?" the star asked him later.

"Well," he replied innocently, "it's true, isn't it?"

Rosie had no doubt about the prudence of protecting him with a bodyguard after the kidnapping threat, but the bodyguard was to create some problems with nervous neighbors later, when Rosie sold the Nyack mansion and bought another country home for her family in exceptionally affluent Fairfield County, Conn.

Some of Rosie's neighbors in Fairfield weren't happy when Parker was escorted to school by an armed bodyguard. They were just as wary as Rosie about guns. Some of the locals grumbled that it was odd that a woman who'd been in a nationally televised battle with Selleck, Heston, and the National Rifle Association about there being too many guns in America would do something as potentially dangerous as sending a man with a handgun to a school.

They didn't mention Columbine.

The complaint distressed Rosie. She'd always been a good neighbor wherever she lived, a helper not a troublemaker. She wanted to be liked and accepted in Connecticut.

Nonetheless, she had a mother's need to assure Parker's security. Just as the neighbors were committed to protecting their young ones, she must protect hers.

Rosie's maternal instincts were in high gear as she was also waiting on a new baby. She'd agreed to adopt a third child, due to be born in January 2000. The doctors were fairly certain the ultrasound exam on the mother showed a girl. The thought of another daughter made Rosie glow.

She was still beaming when the baby was born — a month early — on Dec. 5th. There was a second surprise — the 5-pound, 5-ounce infant was a boy.

"He is the most adorable baby in the world!" Rosie exulted after she saw her new son.

This time, she did something that she hadn't done when she adopted her first two children. The infant's birth mother had asked who was going to adopt, and Rosie agreed to be identified — and also agreed to meet the mother.

"I said, 'Go ahead, tell her it's me,'" Rosie said.

The two women met for a full day, with both of them pleased by the time they parted. "I didn't meet the birth mom when I adopted Parker and Chelsea, so I really didn't know what to expect," Rosie revealed. "But everything went well.

"I know she was pretty surprised. But we spent a day together and did a lot of talking. She is a wonderful, real person who wanted to be sure that her baby was going to a good home."

The birth mother knew she was too young to raise a child but happy to see how loving and baby-wise Rosie O'Donnell was. While Rosie admired the birth mother's courage in yielding the infant so he could have a better life, that was the end of the contact. On December 17, 1999 — a dozen days after he saw daylight — Blake Christopher O'Donnell was officially in Rosie's custody.

As premature babies sometimes do, Blake had arrived with jaundice. His doctors calmed Rosie by assuring her they knew exactly how to take care of that. As she told friends, the medical team did an excellent job by "keeping him under a lamp for a couple of weeks to cure the jaundice, and his condition improved quickly."

When she brought Blake home, Rosie put him near the window, so the sunlight could help finish off the jaundice, and it did. Four-year-old Parker and 2-year-old Chelsea were as delighted as their adoring mother. "They were just overjoyed," Rosie said. "I think they like the idea of having someone around who is smaller than they are."

After giving Blake his first real bath on Christmas morning, she was "happy as a clam. The kids are healthy, they are a delight, and I have a beautiful baby."

After Blake's arrival, Rosie indicated that she wasn't going to stop at three. "I'm taking it one baby at a time, but, yes, I'd love to have more!"

Many parents find the first three months of an infant's life an ordeal, but not Rosie.

"Most people hate it," she said. "They think it's torture. But I love it. I love newborns to death, and little Blake is really cute."

Rosie celebrated the arrival of her blessed Christmas present with Kelli, Parker and Chelsea, while looking forward to a wonderful new year. With everything apparently under control at the studio and in her family, it should have been entirely joyous, but concerns about her own health were to appear on the horizon.

According to a friend, Rosie had taken the fad diet drug fen-phen for a couple of weeks in 1997, when her weight had ballooned to 210. "She had always vowed not to try crazy diet fads, but so many of her friends and co-workers were on it and were achieving miracle results, she thought she'd try it," the friend confided.

"She told me, 'I was so stupid to try this stuff in the first place,'" a pal revealed. "I know now that taking drugs is not an effective way to lose weight. You just have to eat less and exercise more.

"But I have lost sleep at night thinking about what fen-phen may have done to me. Some people have heart defects from taking fen-phen. And I could be one of them."

But she was still overweight, so she went back on a sensible, low-calorie diet with no junk food and some exercise. The dread of a heart attack didn't totally fade. She recalled all the sleep she'd lost worrying about the fen-phen, and that memory was fueled by the pharmaceutical company's offer of nearly $5 billion to 11,000 people who claimed their hearts had been damaged.

The health scares didn't end there.

As the daughter of a woman who died of breast cancer, Rosie also had often worried about whether the disease might take her, too. Her regular, careful breast inspections were reassuring for a while, but then four cysts had been discovered. Concerned that they might lead to cancer, she had welcomed her physician's recommendation that they be surgically removed.

Rosie's vigilant self examinations may have saved her own life, and that same proactive attitude would soon save her daughter, also.

In May, when Chelsea was bitten by a tick at their Fairfield property, and her keen-eyed mother noticed it immediately.

Rosie was on full mother alert the next morning and saw the swollen lymph nodes in Chelsea's neck. Her educated guess was that Chelsea had lyme disease, but still she couldn't help but wonder whether her daughter might be on the way to something even more vicious, maybe lymphoma, a devastating form of cancer.

When the doctor made the diagnosis of lyme disease, Rosie blurted out, "Thank God!"

"What's wrong with you?" he demanded. "She's got lyme disease."

"Yes," relieved Rosie replied, "I thought she might have lymphoma."

While the doctor attacked the lyme effectively with antibiotics, Rosie launched her own plan to prevent any recurrence. Having heard that guinea fowl enjoyed eating ticks, Rosie bought a flock of 37 of the little birds and brought them to her Fairfield home.

Not being an expert on these creatures, she bought adults instead of chicks, which would have stayed in a hen house at first. Before long, eight of the guinea hens had flown the coop . . . over the fence . . . onto nearby properties. One of the confused birds took a run at a sunbathing neighbor, the locals reported.

In the end, Rosie's noble experiment would benefit those who lived nearby, too. In a short time, the fowl would be devouring insects on the neighbor's lawns, leaving them free of ticks, too, expert Jeannette Ferguson told the Enquirer.

Further proving that no good deed goes unpunished, Rosie found herself in a different sort of flap when she spent $75,000 to sponsor her high school reunion in the spring of 2000 — only to find a backlash when her former classmates balked at her banning spouses at the event.

Some of her former pals took to the Internet to voice their displeasure, and former teacher John Ennis revealed that Rosie's reunion rules left "old friends and former high school sweethearts drinking and dancing into the night, in the absence of their wives and husbands. You don't have to be a rocket scientist to realize that is a formula for disaster."

Rosie was shocked at the response. "They weren't even going to have a reunion!" her publicist said of the South Commack alumni. "Rosie was president of her school and homecoming queen. She thought it would be wonderful to tape the reunion with everyone reminiscing. If the spouses were there the whole thing would disintegrate into a 'meeting Rosie session.'"

"People are crazy," said the rebuffed Rosie.

CHAPTER 13

Far removed from the controversy, Rosie and Kelli escaped with the kids to their estate on Star Island, Fla., where they rode the motorcycle, swam, Jet-Skied, and did a bit of fishing. Each trip down south was a refreshing mini-vacation that recharged the batteries of the whole O'Donnell family.

The warm waters off Miami offered so many opportunities for fun and working out — and for helping people, too, as Rosie discovered.

On one occasion, she spotted two young women whom the tide had trapped on a spit of land. They were facing a real threat of being washed away or possibly drowned when she threaded her way up to the rocks on her Jet-Ski to rescue them.

Rosie made no fuss about what she'd done — it seemed like the logical thing for any humane person. She felt the same way about taking in her first foster child, now that she was certified as a foster parent.

The child was a troubled 3-year-old named Mia, who needed a lot of patient caring. Rosie gave Mia, a Hispanic girl with limited English, a great deal of her time.

Having done a great deal of training to become a foster parent, Rosie knew the children she'd be caring for came from backgrounds of neglect and abuse — and worse. But as it turned out, she and the family weren't ready for little Mia.

Mia had been delivered to Rosie from a shelter for abused children in June of 2000, but, no matter how she and the family tried, no amount of soothing words or unabashed love could help little Mia overcome the night terrors that left her wide-awake and screaming in the middle of every night.

"I was up four to five times a night for two weeks," Rosie confided. "It was to the point I was losing my point on the show.

"Mia's had a hard life, and I think she's working it all out when she sleeps. All the unconscious terrors and fears come out."

Rosie had plans to adopt Mia, but after five months, she seemed to be making no headway. The toddler screamed so loudly some times that she frightened the neighbors — who called police!

"It sounds like she's being hurt," Rosie explained. "Which she's not. But she has been and I'm sure she's remembering that. One time she was having one of her screaming fits and a policeman arrived. I opened the door and he gave me this look. I said, 'It's my foster kid. No one is hurting her.'"

Doctors tried to help — one saying Rosie should

tell Mia she would not come to her room, where she slept with lights blazing because of her night fears, until she stopped screaming. "But it took an hour and ten minutes for her to stop screaming," the star revealed.

But Rosie was not going to give up on Mia without a fight — and she had no regrets about her decision to take her — into her home.

"It's the best thing I've ever done in my life, as a person, parent and woman — especially when I think of what that child's life would be like had she not gotten into a loving home."

Rosie's almost endless will to help children, led her on a wild ride that would dominate her thoughts and actions over the next year.

The world learned of it in the fall of 2002, when Rosie had the courage to tell the story in her long-delayed book, "Find Me." Some people would say only a lunatic would get involved in such a bizarre situation. Others say only Rosie could get into such a fantastic web of intrigue.

She already had more than enough on her mind with the nonstop work of "The Rosie O'Donnell Show" and her entertainment career and her many time-consuming projects to help those who needed it. She was as devoted to and busy with her four small children as any mother in America. Add to all this another endeavor — the development of a new monthly magazine to be named "Rosie."

The powerhouse conglomerate that owned McCall's, a German megafirm named Gruner and Jahr, was enthusiastic about partnering with the multitalented talk-show star and actress. The idea was to drastically remake and to reinvigorate McCall's under the very popular name of "Rosie."

What appealed to Rosie was that she'd have a significant say in the whole "look," as another talented and wealthy talk-show queen based in Chicago had with her monthly.

The magazine "Oprah" was a success, and Rosie liked the idea of having her own success in print. She'd been a success in television, film, nightclubs and theater, including an acclaimed recent turn in an offbeat Broadway musical. After performing so well in "Seussical," based on a best-selling series of children's books, and glittering as the happy sassy hostess of the Tony Awards twice, Rosie was ready for new career adventures.

While the multimillion-dollar magazine project was getting off the ground, another adventure was coming at her out of the blue. She'd finally decided to leave the complex and uncomfortable life in Fairfield County, Conn. Her focus was on a new home in a place that surprised both friends and fans.

Word came that Rosie was indeed about to move with Kelli and their three adopted children to familiar Rockland County north of New York City. That was where she'd lived in Nyack in the former Helen Hayes mansion. Her new place was an easy drive from the Manhattan studio and her town-house, and the stores and eating weren't nearly as grand and pricey as those in posh Fairfield County, the most fashionable area in Connecticut.

Rosie has never left her roots in certain ways. She can be happy with chili dogs, Ring Dings and burgers. While she's learned how to dress "up" for awards ceremonies and charity balls, she doesn't need costly designer gowns and is often seen in the casual, inexpensive clothes that a gym teacher might wear and can be bought at a Target or K-mart.

While she housed her children in luxurious homes and bought top-quality furniture, and she didn't deny herself a speedboat and Jet-Ski in Florida and had the newest computers, Rosie didn't lose touch with the great masses of regular people — especially women — who made her talk show such a huge and profitable success.

As she's often said, Rosie's never lost track of the fact that family and children are more important to her than money and fame. While superstars such as Barbra Streisand left Rosie almost speechless, the talk-show host admitted that her real heroine was Mia Farrow, the elfin movie actress whose commitment to raising and loving children included adopting from several countries. Mia has adopted an even dozen children.

That Rosie's dreams were beginning to change must have been sensed by the executives at Warner Brothers' television syndication. Although she didn't say there was a shift in her thinking, the corporate veterans were no doubt aware that the future of "The Rosie O'Donnell Show" was uncertain.

They liked Rosie, and they'd coddled her in a thousand ways to keep the star happy and the sponsors willing to continue paying millions for commercials on her unique talk show. Although her contract wouldn't run out for well over a year, they "casually" suggested they'd like to renew and extend it for several more years.

They didn't have to say they'd pay her an even huger salary. That's a given in the television business.

Although her contract wasn't about to run out, Rosie was giving serious thought to letting it do just that. They couldn't believe that a "hot" performer, a woman in her 30s supporting several small children and a lover who'd left her own corporate job, could walk away from a future that would pay over $20 million each year. It defied all the rules of show business.

She wouldn't dare, they told themselves.

The star had a unique personality and an offbeat approach to life, the "suits" reasoned sensibly, but she wasn't defiant enough to blow it all. This talk that she might not renew was probably just a negotiating tactic, they figured, so they'd let some time go by and come back for the next round of contract talks in due course.

After all, Rosie didn't seem angry or even in a bad mood. She had no complaints about the staff now, and she was finding satisfaction in her philanthropic works. Almost all her projects were to help young children, and one of the main ones was For All Children, the foundation she'd started herself and still helped with major contributions.

If she abandoned the talk show, she'd have much less cash flow to fund the foundation, the Warner realists told themselves. Once again, they assured each other that she wouldn't dare.

For the previous year, Rosie's weekly routine had included devoting one afternoon to an adoption "meeting" — which focused on helping children in need find homes.

One May afternoon, Rosie met with a counselor named Colleen who began to go down the list of who had called, who had returned the forms properly completed, and what the problem cases might be.

"It was pretty standard fare until she opened a blue folder on her lap," Rosie recalled.

Then Colleen gasped, "Oh, God. This is so sad." Colleen, who was no beginner, began to cry.

Unable to help herself, Rosie was instantly in what she calls "savior mode."

A 14-year-old girl named Stacie had been raped by a youth minister. She was in shock and pregnant. Her mother had telephoned on the hotline offered on Rosie's show and said she felt the baby should be "placed for adoption" but would accept whatever her daughter decided.

Rosie had learned it was unwise for her to get personally involved in the process. She knew she shouldn't communicate with the pregnant girl's mother, but the terrible tragedy of this situation made her break her rule.

Involved? No. As she revealed in "Find Me," she became overinvolved — impulsively and immediately. She grabbed the phone and dialed the number of the rape victim's mother, hearing an assured female voice on an answering machine.

She left a message. "Hi, this is Rosie O'Donnell. If I can be of any help, please call. Anything — we can provide financial aid for counseling. I know this must be horrible for you and your daughter, and I'm very sorry it happened."

After she returned the mother's call, Rosie went to a scheduled therapy session with her "no-nonsense shrink." When she told the whole story to her therapist who'd heard so many intense and true personal stories from her famous and lonely patient, the doctor answered thoughtfully.

"Ro, you have to learn to sit on your hands," she said.

It was caring advice Rosie had heard from her many times, and would hear again.

Rosie wondered then as she does now whether her need to save people is good or bad. She still finds the line between compulsion and compassion often blurred. "Are artists driven by creativity or insanity?" she has asked, trying to understand and accept Roseann O'Donnell, who hasn't entirely left Commack.

But there is more at work within Rosie's psyche, says psychiatrist Dr. Carole Lieberman. "Underneath Rosie's Queen of Nice exterior is a controlling woman trying to get out," Lieberman told the Enquirer. "When her mother died, Rosie's childhood became chaotic and completely out of control. So she's wanted to control things — even others' troubled lives."

Rosie kept revisiting the mental-health issues in the Stacie episode — her own as well as those of the raped adolescent and the abused child's mother.

"On a good day, I think I'm a relatively sane person with a few frayed wires," Rosie once wrote. "On a bad day, I think, 'just lock me up.' "

On the day after Rosie returned the mother's appeal, the star wondered whether she'd ever hear back. Then, a staffer at the show found her and said, "Some kid's on the phone. She said you gave her this number."

Picking up the receiver, Rosie heard the voice of a child. It was flat and dull, but that wasn't what mattered. What mattered was this was Stacie.

"My mom said I should call."

"Thanks for calling. My name is Rosie, and I'll help you any way I can."

And the sophisticated Emmy-winning star slid right into a world as unreal as the "wonderland" Alice found when she went through that legendary looking-glass.

Stacie called Rosie back with something more urgent a few nights later at half past eleven. Rosie's caller ID showed the area code of a West Coast location.

"I don't want no baby," the girl announced.

She was afraid of possible pain in birth and doubtful when Rosie tried to reassure her that good doctors could make the discomfort minimal and adoption by good people would be no problem at all.

Stacie's next call for help and human contact came at three in the morning.

"I can't sleep," the girl reported. "I'm sad. My best friend isn't talking to me anymore. We had this fight. What kind of kid were you?"

Off guard and groggy, the motherless star let it all hang out to this distant stranger.

"You sound really sad," the rape victim consoled. "Don't be sad."

Strange as this conversation was, the relationship was to get a lot stranger. Soon Stacie was telephoning several times a week, late at night. In the morning, concerned Rosie would call the girl's mother to let her know "what was up" without going into details.

Rosie wanted to protect the teenager. A new element came into the difficult mix when Barbara, the mother, reported that husband Doug was "very distressed" about the daughter's plight. Rosie, who has admitted that she knows no boundaries and gets into trouble because of her impetuosity, offered to speak to Doug.

Over the sounds of children in the background, Rosie heard that Barbara doubted he'd come to the phone because he was "kind of grumpy and shy."

As the late-night talks with Stacie continued, Rosie began to notice small shifts in the teenager's voice and personality. In the blackness of the night, Rosie grasped that "Stacie had many sides, shifts and splits in her, as I had in me."

In one call, the mother said other children were taunting Stacie about her swelling belly and wondered whether it might not be best to move the pregnant teenager away from these pressures out there in Oregon.

Concerned, Rosie said she'd pay to bring Stacie to New Jersey and find a suitable place for the girl to stay until the baby arrived.

Seconds after the call ended, Rosie was on the phone with her high-powered attorney, asking whether there might possibly be any legal issues involved in moving a pregnant minor across state lines.

After warning Rosie that Stacie might not actually

be pregnant and it might all be a story to get money from the compassionate and generous Rosie O'Donnell, he said her idea was not illegal. With permission of a parent, she could come across as many state lines as the family approved.

Rosie charged right on, calling friends and relatives to try to find housing and a 24-hour caregiver for the rape victim. Stacie's mother had to stay in Oregon with her four other children, Rosie explained hopefully. When no one agreed to take Stacie, Rosie decided she'd handle it herself.

With the show on hiatus, Rosie and her family plus Kelli would be basking in Florida for months. The pregnant teenager could bunk in the Manhattan townhouse. Pushing the envelope as she usually did, the star persuaded a personal friend to quit her job and come take care of Stacie. She'd be well paid.

As she recalled in "Find Me," she was pleased that she'd solved the problem. But Rosie did a lot more thinking about why she was drawn to this victimized child.

It was a sense of shared pain, she discovered.

And she realized that she liked it.

The calls kept Rosie deeply involved. A well-educated friend of hers was at her house one night and heard a message that Stacie had left on the answering machine. The Ivy League graduate told Rosie that it didn't sound like a 14-year-old's voice. Of course, Rosie wouldn't listen to this cynicism.

Stacie's situation worsened. Her mother phoned to say that she'd begun to bleed. Rosie nearly panicked.

"She's very weak and the doctor is worried," Barbara continued before she began to weep.

Rosie's concern and generosity escalated. She invited the teenager and her mother to come down to Miami for a weekend "when this is all over." Rosie would supply the airline tickets, or she'd fly west to see them.

Crisis followed crisis. While Stacie's medical state was better, her mental condition suddenly "went kerphooey," and the tragic teenager was transferred to the psychiatric ward on the hospital's 7th floor.

Rosie considered flying right out to see her, hesitated, and then sent her a phone card so Stacie could call at no cost. Rosie worried day and night. It was hard to focus on other things. She tried to escape for a few hours to work on the art of creative paper cutting and collage in her craft room. Decoupage was one of Rosie's favorite outlets for her imagination, but it didn't work this time.

She sent Stacie lots of presents, but they didn't help. The abused teenager was catatonic most of the time, crying the rest. She wouldn't be well enough to come east, her mother said, so the baby would probably be born in the psychiatric ward. Depressed by this and worn out with a cold, Rosie wasn't her usual positive self a day or two later, when her Ivy League friend, Carolyn Strauss, came by to visit.

The conversation soon turned to the rape victim. Rosie was indignant when skeptical Carolyn said she'd like to speak with Stacie herself. "She's been through enough already," Rosie replied.

Rosie's friend would not back off. She proposed they call the hospital to find out if Stacie was registered. It was a ridiculous thought. "Bournewood," Rosie said, naming the hospital in a tone that suggested her doubting friend was "an Ivy League moron."

Rosie finally called the hospital number that Barbara had provided. When a voice answered "Bournewood," the star hung up in breathless anxiety. She wasn't pleased when her friend pointed out that she hadn't asked if Stacie was registered. Her friend still wasn't convinced that everything was what it seemed.

Now Rosie pointed out that neither child nor mother had asked for money or accepted the cash she offered. Rosie felt that should settle suspicions of impropriety.

Some people won't take no or even "maybe" for an answer.

Carolyn is one of those difficult individuals. It may have been all that education, but she wasn't convinced. Rosie shrugged this off, for she had so much more to do for Stacie. Being practical, she decided to seek help for the girl from a social agency in the pregnant teen's hometown in Oregon.

She told the whole story to a social worker out there, a sensible-sounding woman named Janice. Rosie, who'd learned the lingo of the adoption world, asked Janice to "do an intake" on Friday. The social worker was persuaded to agree to meet the mother of the young woman who was about to deliver.

News of more problems arrived in phone calls from the Oregon hospital. It was up and down for Stacie. First a nurse phoned to say she seemed to be getting better, but really bad news followed. A sonogram showed within the rape victim a little dead girl.

The mother was sobbing. Poor Stacie endured seven awful hours of labor. Then Rosie learned that the baby had been stillborn. Stacie hadn't wanted to see her, Barbara reported.

It was finally over, Rosie thought.

She had no idea of what was coming the next morning.

CHAPTER 14

ROSIE DID WHAT A CARING AND RESPONSIBLE ADULT WOULD DO.

Aware that the social worker in Oregon would be just about ready to depart from her office to meet Stacie and arrange the intake, Rosie telephone to advise her not to bother.

"The adoption's off," the concerned celebrity said. "The baby died."

"I don't know how to tell you," the social worker began. "There is no baby. There never was."

There was no record of any pregnant teenager at that hospital. No record of a Barb and Doug Davis in Ashland, Oregon, or elsewhere in the state.

"There is no Stacie," the social worker concluded. "I've looked and looked and turned up nothing. I'm sorry, Rosie. This has all been a hoax."

Rosie didn't believe it. This was impossible, she told herself for the next few hours as she stared in mute shock at the ceiling. There must be more to this story, she assured herself. She felt it — absolutely.

She couldn't simply accept what she'd heard, so she went back to her phone to call the police station in Ashland. First the woman who answered doubted that it was the TV star Rosie O'Donnell on the line. Rosie insisted, told a concise version of the Stacie story and asked whether there might be a Stacie and Barbara Davis in Ashland and whether they might have criminal records.

The police in Ashland wouldn't give any information, and Rosie wouldn't give up her quest. She had to know. She was a determined and wholly modern detective with an expensive computer. Yahoo might have an answer.

She made a start. There was a 7 Hysink Road in Ashland. So the address existed. But did Barbara Davis? The stubborn star typed that name into the question box on the screen.

Bingo. Barbara Davis in Anaheim, Calif.

Rosie called information for the number and dialed it. She heard a barking dog, then the voice of a very old woman.

"Yes, I'm Barb-ar-a," she croaked. "Who is this?"

The star panicked and hung up the phone. That aged person hadn't sounded anything like Stacie's mother. Baffled as to who this woman might be, Rosie redialed the Ashland police station to ask whether they had even any record at all — forget the names — of a 14-year-old girl raped by a youth minister.

"No, and I've lived here all my life," the woman on duty answered. When Rosie gave her the "Davis" phone number she'd been dialing for months, the TV star got another shock.

That phone number belonged to a 38-year-old woman named Melissa Star. The Ashland police knew her address. "We're familiar with it," the officer said cautiously.

Rosie found that vague enough to drive her "out of her mind," so she punched the number she'd been calling for months into her phone one more time.

She heard a strange flat voice she remembers as "weirder than weird." The woman didn't seem bothered that Rosie knew she was Melissa, and didn't appear convinced she was talking to Rosie O'Donnell "from TV."

"Who is this? Mindy? Dawn?" she tested.

Rosie had a hunch, and she played it. She asked this Melissa if she was seeing "a shrink." The stranger showed no tension as she said yes, rattling off the therapist's phone number and name. Melissa said she didn't mind if Rosie phoned her.

Therapist Tina Lano wouldn't confirm that she treated Melissa Star. Lano had never heard of O'Donnell or her talk show, but she took the phone number in New York so she could call back. Now Rosie had another hunch — wilder than the previous one. It was the only explanation she could imagine.

"Is she a multiple?"

"I'll call you tomorrow," the therapist replied coolly.

Once more, the star was reminded how frail fame is. Lano hadn't heard of "The Rosie O'Donnell Show," either, but her son verified who Rosie was and mysterious Melissa had told the therapist she could spell out the whole story.

There was no Stacie or Barbara Davis. Melissa Star had multiple personality disorder, as Rosie guessed. Her "alters" were Stacie and Barb and Doug, and there was a Nancy and a Kate and several others. Since Melissa had lost her job a few months ago, she'd been severely depressed, causing the various personalities to resurface.

Without hesitation, without thinking, Rosie impulsively wanted to help. She offered to give money or set up a trust fund.

"Why would you give money to a person you don't know?" the therapist asked thoughtfully.

Rosie answered the question with a question. Why did she feel she had to help the whole world?

Lano's reply was complete and powerful.

"Narcissism. You think you're powerful enough to change things. It keeps you from having to really work on yourself."

The therapist returned to the multiple. Melissa had been battered psychologically by such severe childhood traumas that she could cope only by splitting into separate selves. After she briefly described some of these horrors, Rosie couldn't help offering to help again.

Rosie's body already showed how deeply involved she was with the damaged Stacie. Before the revelation of the multiple personalities, Rosie was mentally sharing the pain she believed the imaginary teenager felt. She had returned to a tattoo artist with extraordinary instructions.

Replace the pretty flowers with "grit and gears" she had said. "Make my skin look ripped, revealing gears underneath like a machine with vines growing through the chaos in defiance," she said. She was determined to bond with the hurt of the teenager, and to show it.

After all the years as a funny, rich and famous adult, Rosie still hadn't broken free of a sad need to suffer. Six hours of tattooing left her leg throbbing with the "sought-out suffering" she loved, the star admitted in her 2002 confessional "Find Me."

The complex Rosie-Stacie-Melissa story was far from over. The intense talk-show star somehow couldn't let go. She had to stay in touch with Melissa. Sending the splintered woman out in Ashland an expensive new computer made a steady flow of e-mails easy. Rosie's frank explanation for this stubbornness was a touching thing.

She couldn't stop hoping.

"At no point did the girl I'd come to love emerge," the celebrity finally recognized. "I missed her, my little Stacie. I ended up meeting the others."

The messages from "the others" weren't easy to deal with, for some of the e-mails seethed with hate and some spoke of self-mutilation and hurting. Rosie remembered her own harsh hurting as a child enough so she could relate. Her odd relationship with the sick person she'd come to call "my multiple" was getting addictive. The e-mails were taking priority over almost everyone except her children and Kelli.

Many of Rosie's friends were beginning to worry about her. Carolyn, who'd been skeptical about Stacie from way back, was now insisting that her friend stop the communication and relation with the multiple.

Rosie then consulted a friend who was a therapist. Confirming what she'd heard, he told her that most multiples were women abused in childhood, and gave her many case histories with experiences she recognized, because many "splits" still survived in her.

Then she found herself answering a very important question.

No, she wasn't a multiple.

She looked inside and judged that all the parts of Roseann O'Donnell — the adult woman she called Ro — had remained "integrated, connected, aware of each other." She concluded that a central Rosie was always present, and that knowing how to help herself made her "a definite I" who was different from Melissa.

Was that the end of it?

It could have been. It should have been. It wasn't.

Soon afterward, Rosie was starring on Broadway in the youth-oriented "Seussical" musical. During the rehearsals, the famous actress-entertainer-talk-show host had lit up with one of those unusual Rosie ideas. Her friends agreed unanimously that it was "nuts" and said so.

It was February now, nine months after Rosie "met" Melissa on the phone. Suddenly her curiosity intensified, and she wanted to meet Melissa face to face in New York. It would be a thrilling adventure, Rosie exulted. Therapist Tina should come, too, so Melissa wouldn't be uncomfortable or alone in unfamiliar New York City.

Rosie convinced the woman in Oregon that seeing Rosie singing and dancing in a big Broadway musical would be great fun. The star planned it all carefully. Using airline tickets she provided, they flew in from Oregon on Thursday night to a New York airport, where Rosie's "hippie surfer-dude" driver met them and brought them in his limousine to the mid-Manhattan hotel.

When a nervous Rosie went to her TV studio Friday morning, therapist and patient were waiting backstage. Tina was a smiling, attractive woman in her 60s, calm and reassuring. With fear in her face and telltale burns of self-hurting on her hands, dark-haired Melissa was shy and wary until Rosie hugged her.

Bigger than the star and wearing glasses, she was Rosie's age and visibly uncomfortable at first. The tension eased when she thanked Rosie and smiled in appreciation. Rosie had to go on stage for the telecast. As soon as she spotted them seated in the audience, she was distracted throughout the whole show. Her sense that only a thin line separated them was acute.

After the cameras went dark, the three women met in Rosie's private office for sandwiches and small talk about the flight and hotel. Both experiences were wholly new to Melissa. Then, the therapist acted to unite the three of them in common bond. She gave Rosie and Melissa each an identical Indian change purse, beaded and holding a small stone carved with a message of uplift.

It represented faith and trust, she told them as she held both of them by the hand. For the rest of the weekend they came together at meals and at the theater, where Rosie glittered as The Cat in the Hat in "Seussical."

The troubled visitor proved to be nice, normal, and really ordinary to Rosie, who expected something more. This wasn't the fantasy Melissa whom Rosie had "fallen for" — the woman who had created Stacie. She wasn't Rosie's intriguing multiple anymore, the star thought after they were gone.

Rosie now saw the truth . . . another truth. There was nothing to bind her to Melissa now that Rosie knew her. The motherless star had to accept the fact that there was no longer any Stacie in her life.

Rosie's recollection of that important moment of self-awareness and recognition was so clear she could put it in a few words.

"Now I had nothing left between me and me," she thought.

It was a turning point she wouldn't forget.

It was a step forward that offered a chance for a different life.

CHAPTER 15

Even with the incredible Stacie-Melissa fantasy finally over, there was ongoing tension in the life of dynamic Rosie O'Donnell. She didn't seem to look for it, but it came to her as it had for so many years. A stress-free existence was never going to happen for this big and adventurous woman.

The challenges just kept coming at her.

In one fell swoop in 2001, she lived through a cancer nightmare, lost her beloved-but-troubled foster daughter Mia — and then nearly lost her hand when what seemed like a simple knife cut became infected.

"Things have to get better," Rosie lamented. "Because they can't get much worse than what has happened to me this spring."

Because of her mother's premature death, plus the death at 39 of a friend from ovarian cancer, Rosie had gone in to her doctor for her annual ultrasound screening for ovarian cancer in late March. Doctors found tumors and, unsure if they were benign or cancerous, told Rosie they wanted to go in and take them out. "I absolutely froze when they told me they'd found tumors that could be cancer," she admitted.

"Cancer is a word no one wants to hear from their doctor," Rosie said. "I was terrified. I may not be the most religious woman in the world, but I did pray: 'OK, God, I'm leaving it up to you. Just bring me through this.'"

The day after the ultrasound, doctors went into Rosie's abdomen and removed the tumors. Tests proved they were not malignant. "I was lying groggily in the recovery room when my doctor came in, roused me, and said, 'Rosie! Rosie, no cancer! It doesn't look like cancer!'" she recalled.

However, "The doctors found and removed four tumors along with both fallopian tubes, part of an ovary and some uterine lining," Rosie said. If she'd harbored any latent thoughts about conceiving a child the old-fashioned way — and she says she hadn't — those dreams were now shattered.

Another dream — that of raising troubled Mia as part of the family — also was shattered at about the same time Rosie went through her cancer scare.

Rosie had tried everything to soothe the little girl and incorporate her into her family. But in March 2001, doctors told Rosie that the little girl needed to be placed in a facility that could care for her special needs. The loss of Mia echoed the travails of her Stacie episode — and was a bitter blow to the woman who sincerely wants to ease the ills of every child in the world.

"People said I was crazy to take in a child with such

problems, and I probably am," Rosie admitted. "I think I can save everyone. It's my weakness and my strength. But is it compassion or compulsion?

"From the beginning, there were difficulties. For months she woke up screaming in fear at night. She also hurt herself sometimes, scratching her arms to the point where they would bleed and require bandaging. And at meals she would hide food in her clothes, as if she was afraid she would never have enough."

"There were also incidents with my other children," Rosie confided. "Mia never attacked them — she's not the demon seed. But there were real concerns with my baby, Blakie.

"Once, when I gave Mia a piece of butterscotch sucking candy, she asked if I could give it to Blake. I told her no and explained that babies like Blake can choke to death on hard candy. But as soon as I turned my back I heard Blake choking and had to race over and pull the candy from his mouth.

"Every time an incident occurred, minor or major, I — as a foster parent — was required to file a detailed report to Mia's doctors," Rosie said. "Finally they told me they felt it was time for her to come in for more evaluation and 24-hour-a-day treatment."

Rosie said she would continue to pray that Mia would one day be allowed back into her family. "But no matter what happens," she said, "I love Mia very much. If the doctors say she can't come back into this family, I've already found two families that will take her so that I can be there for her as an aunt."

Rosie said she had enough small triumphs

with Mia to make it all worth the struggle.

"Every night I would tell Mia in Spanish that I loved her and she would say 'uh-uh' and turn her head and close her eyes," she said. "Then finally in January, after months of this, she whispered to me in English, 'I love you, Mama' with her eyes closed. I was crying. From then on she'd whisper it to me every night. I can't describe how much that means to me. It is beautiful.

"Now that she's away at the facility she sleeps with one of my T-shirts scented with my perfume, CK One. I phone her every day. Whatever happens, I will always be a part of Mia's life."

But there were other things at work below the surface of Rosie's struggles to take care of — and adopt — Mia.

It had never crossed Rosie's mind that Kelli's being part of her household might disturb the state officials. The first three children had been adopted in New York, where everything went smoothly. Rosie's love life wasn't an issue to child care authorities and the courts up in the Empire State.

Rosie's commitment to a female partner hadn't been that well-known to the public when the first three children were adopted. Perhaps even more important, the statutes and regulations covering adoption in New York were different from those in Florida. New York didn't hold a parent's sexuality as a test to be passed. Rosie wasn't really conscious of the fact that it was a law in Florida. It was on the statute books after debate and formal approval by the state legislature and signature by the governor.

You could look it up, if you wanted to.

Rosie couldn't and didn't because she didn't know the law existed. Before she found out, state authorities officially told her to return Mia to the care of a social agency that could give her the additional psychiatric and other attention that her condition still needed.

Rosie hadn't been able to let go of her connection with the imaginary Stacie, and now she wouldn't abandon her link with the real and troubled Mia. Rosie had no difficulty bonding with troubled individuals — especially young females. Whether she identified with them or not, she cared so much for Mia that she pressed for visitation rights and told the state that she could still help her.

If Mia couldn't live with Rosie, the star insisted, this "special" girl needed especially caring parents for either foster care or adoption. Rosie was ready to propose the names of two Florida couples she thought fit the bill.

Rosie was shocked by what she discovered next.

Florida's statute and regulations permitted gay people to serve as foster parents but barred them from adopting. As Richard Mintzer's 2003 report on adoption in the United States shows, there were three states that had and enforced prohibitions to prevent gay adoptions. The two, besides Florida, were Mississippi and Utah.

Rosie didn't know about the Florida statute, and she had no idea that a number of the 49 states that didn't bar gay adoptions were listening to appeals that they change their policies and laws. It isn't a subject that many people talk about . . . not a "hot" button issue, like abortion or gun control. That may be why executives at the Nickelodeon TV channel — where Kelli Carpenter had worked — didn't expect the more than 200,000 complaints that poured in after it broadcast a half-hour documentary on gay adoption.

Quick-witted and more than stubborn, Rosie made two decisions in short order. The first dealt with the legal barrier. She couldn't deal with the pressures to pass more anti-gay adoption legislation in other states, but she could concentrate on the situation in Florida.

She would launch a drive to change the law.

Convinced that it was backward-looking and unfair, she would support a new law to be introduced via a public drive or referendum. She'd have to do this at the right time and with the support of non-gay allies. She'd argue that the current statute was discriminatory; she'd seek the backing of the American Civil Liberties Union.

She hoped the ACLU would see this as an issue of principle, knowing that it was used to taking chances for what it saw as principles. It had offended many people with its unpopular positions, so the fact that a great number of men and women had made clear they opposed gay couples adopting might not put off the ACLU.

But Rosie soon had other battles to fight.

Shortly after giving up Mia for professional treatment, Rosie had a huge scare to go with her heartache.

She suffered a small knife wound on her left palm while cutting the price tag off of a fishing pole. Fixing the cut required surgery because of a severed nerve — and Rosie hardly found the cut worth mentioning.

"Then the surgical repair ruptured and I needed another operation," she disclosed. "Then scar tissue formed in the wound and I needed still another operation. One morning after the final surgery I woke up in agony. The hand was red and swollen and felt like it had a hot poker jammed inside."

The wound, originally a small cut, had developed a dangerous staph infection — and Rosie's doctors were talking about amputation. "I wound up going to the hospital and spending a week in ICU!" Rosie went on. "First the doctors said they might have to take my middle finger. Then they said they might have to take the whole hand to save my life. It was really scary. I was afraid I was dying. I told them, 'Do whatever you have to do, but I don't want to die.'"

Fortunately, antibiotics ultimately won out over the infection, and Rosie's hand — and life — was spared. Through the entire ordeal, Kelli had slept by Rosie's side on the floor of the intensive care unit — an act of selflessness and love that would lead to the couple taking the next big step in their relationship.

In the midst of all this turmoil — the cancer scare, losing Mia, facing amputation — Rosie was presented with a business offer she couldn't refuse.

Rosie had never carried a daily talk show before she started her own in 1996, and yet she'd made it a big fat cash cow that captivated a huge national audience and major advertisers. Of course, the veteran production people of the Warner television syndication group played important roles, but it was Rosie who made it happen.

Now, after almost five years of daytime success on stations across the country, Rosie was ready to star in another medium. Long before Oprah, her friend and gifted rival, had launched a new monthly that carried her name, Roseann O'Donnell had been an enthusiastic reader who was fascinated by the world of print. She was in a way typical of her generation — devoted television watchers in their youth who secretly respected the written word as somehow more classical and serious.

She was wide open for a new world to conquer when two men came to her with the idea of her very own monthly magazine. There's little doubt that Phillip K. Howard, one of her league of lawyers, and Dan Crimmins, her business manager-accountant, sincerely believed that it made sense to start a magazine named Rosie in partnership with a big publishing syndicate that had deep pockets.

While they were practical men who knew how business works, they were also well acquainted with Rosie. Crimmins was married to her sister and had known Rosie for years. He had to be aware that she was highly talented and had great intelligence with a short-fused temper.

Crimmins admired and respected his rich, multitalented and famous sister-in-law who was remarkable in many ways. There were also ways in which she was like a lot of other people. If something went wrong, Rosie was one of the mere mortals who'd blame somebody else.

Crimmins and Howard approached the idea of the magazine carefully. Rosie had already made it clear she'd had enough of the television talk show after four plus years, even though it had made her a star and earned her $120 million. They had also collected smaller but very significant sums and would continue to do that if they came up with another cash-cow venture for her.

They brought in a consultant, an expert in magazine publishing with big-league experience that could help shape a plan that would convince some group with cash and a taste for magazines to join in the project. The consultant was brainy and with-it Annalyn Swan, a sophisticated Manhattanite who had an excellent sense of today's potential readers as well as an appreciation of numbers.

Being well plugged in and aware of what a strong — often tempestuous, but appealingly fresh — individual Rosie had shown herself to be, Ms. Swan was attracted to the possibility of shaping a magazine to reflect Rosie's colorful and down-to-earth personality.

Like Rosie, it would be different. It would aim at women readers, but it wouldn't be like the existing ones that offered them little else but beauty tips, diet stuff, and fluffy articles and air-brushed photos of the world of glamour. The magazine community and its "suits" weren't up on Rosie O'Donnell's well-earned reputation as a stubborn individual who could be tough on anyone who didn't agree with her sometimes impulsive judgments.

Rosie had risen the hard way, and she thought that what mattered was real people and their concerns — not lipsticks or starlets. She wasn't the world's greatest team player or manager, and her organizational skills were less than superb.

She wanted to help or inspire people, not sell them.

The small team designing the prototype of a first issue to show potential partners and the all-powerful advertising agencies knew they had to shape two presentations in terms of the basic concept.

To get the magazine off the ground so it could grow into something that everyone would like, they had to talk about it one way to Rosie O'Donnell and another to the hard-boiled corporate interests that could make it a reality. Nobody was trying to fool anyone. Swan, the lawyer and business manager, honestly believed they could reconcile these differences and succeed.

They had some time to fine-tune and sweet-talk.

Rosie wasn't closing her talk show until spring 2002. The magazine could be up to speed by then, offering her an outlet for her creative energies, a forum for her views that had interested millions of TV viewers, and a new investment that would pay her handsomely.

It was an accident waiting to happen.

After plenty of highly professional polishing, a prototype and proposal were offered to big organizations that might have the money and will to float "Rosie" — the magazine. Time, Inc. was the first to say no. Then Primedia took a "pass," and so did several others.

Finally it went to the publishing company Gruner & Jahr, which belongs to the huge German media firm Bertelsmann, which also owns the major U.S. book publisher Random House and the powerful BMG music group. Its main magazine properties were

"Parents," "Family Circle," "YM," and 125-year-old "McCall's," which was ailing. Circulation was down to 4,250,000 — a loss of 500,000 in the past year.

Instead of starting from scratch, the thought that finally emerged was to build on the existing circulation of "McCall's" and stop the $2 million a month loss by offering a peppy new magazine titled "Rosie's McCall's." It would have a fresh and lively attitude, and the twin benefits of Rosie's input and her name.

The input would be both editorial and financial. In terms of money and ownership, O'Donnell would invest $6 million for half of the venture. Gruner & Jahr agreed to pitch in a lot more than that.

With her magazine still young but promising, Rosie was considering when she might make the move that Ellen DeGeneres and several other lesbian women in entertainment had been urging her to make for years. She'd been reluctant to acknowledge that she loved females, concerned that it might outrage her many fans in middle America who had different values. She hadn't wished to risk angering them or her show's advertisers.

Looking back, Rosie found it hard to believe that most of her fans were, indeed, hoodwinked on the issue of her sexuality.

"I had a meeting with Warner Bros. eight years ago, at the age of 32, before starting the show and said, 'I want you to know I'm gay, and I want you to be OK with the fact that I'm gay,'" she told the gay publication "The Advocate" in 2002. "I want to be upfront at the beginning."

She said she lived her life "as though everyone knew" she was gay.

"Look, I'm sitting on a plane and the flight attendant goes, 'Hi, Rosie — oh, my God, my partner's name is Frank, and I just love you, love your show.' I'm sitting next to Kelli, and we both wear matching rings — it's pretty obvious to everyone who's gay.

"There were many people who said to me, 'Famous or not, why don't you come out?' and I always said, 'I'm out enough,' because I never pretended to have a boyfriend."

It would become even more obvious once the show was out of the way — and Rosie was seeing to it that that obstacle would be removed before too long.

In a stunning move, Rosie had already informed the syndication company that she would not continue the highly profitable daily talk show after mid-spring in 2002, and word was seeping out to her loyal coast-to-coast TV audience. But when there was no show, there'd be no audience or advertisers to lose. With that danger gone, she could push the drive to get the Florida law changed without worrying that it might expose her sexuality.

There were, of course, two large groups who'd known about Rosie O'Donnell's love life for years. One was the in-crowd in show business. The other consisted of readers of the National Enquirer. In fact, when the celebrated talk-show host eventually came out as gay, the front-page story in "USA Today" mentioned that the Enquirer had the secret story first.

It quoted Patrick Spreng, a savvy Rosie authority who had written an early biography of her, as being "sure the National Enquirer is doubled over laughing, because they've been saying this for years with pictures and everything."

CHAPTER 16

IN ADDITION TO CONSIDERING A TIMETABLE FOR ATTACKING THE FLORIDA LAW, ROSIE AND KELLI NOW AGREED TO MOVE AHEAD WITH ANOTHER EVEN MORE IMPORTANT MATTER. WHETHER THEY SUCCEEDED IN GETTING FLORIDA'S VOTERS, A DIVERSE GROUP THAT INCLUDED MANY CONSERVATIVE-MINDED SENIOR CITIZENS WHO'D RETIRED TO THE SUNSHINE STATE, TO CHANGE THE LAW WOULD NOT STOP ROSIE AND KELLI FROM ADDING ANOTHER INFANT TO THE FAMILY.

Adoption wasn't the only way.

The couple could do an end run around the prohibition in the Florida law if Kelli had a baby — the old-fashioned way.

Kelli welcomed the idea. She was in her 30s, so if she was to have a baby she might as well do it before too long. A person close to the couple reported that Kelli immediately approved Rosie's suggestion in late 2001 that they now go forward with what they'd talked about for more than a year.

But first, Rosie and Kelli decided to get married.

Several years before, Rosie had run for the hills when her then-lover Michelle Blakely said she wanted to wed Rosie. She wasn't ready, and she knew America wasn't ready to learn she was in a committed lesbian relationship.

But now the gloves were off. Rosie was coming out of the closet — she wasn't sure exactly when, but with the show already scheduled to end in May 2002, it was just a matter of time — and she was open to the idea of marrying Kelli.

Rosie was dropping hints about her sexual orientation. Accepting a Daytime Emmy earlier that year, Rosie in her acceptance speech professed her love for Kelli.

Rosie's litany of crises that year — the loss of Mia, the cancer scare, the prospect of losing a hand — brought them closer together than ever. Kelli had been Rosie's rock throughout the ordeals — and Rosie had fallen even deeper in love with Kelli as the year progressed.

"Kelli is the perfect mate for Rosie," a source revealed. "Rosie is filled with insecurities and Kelli is very nurturing and patient with her. She's helping Rosie work through the deep-seated issues that have given her clinical depression and other problems. I think Rosie feels truly loved for the first time since her mother died."

Another source said that despite her earlier relationship with Michelle Blakely and her fling with nanny Kate Fitzgerald, "Rosie was lonely for a long time. She dated a lot of women but never found her soul mate until Kelli came along."

Over the summer of 2001, they discussed traveling

to Vermont, where same-sex marriages are legal. But Rosie and Kelli ultimately decided to have a simple ceremony where their hearts were — at home, with the kids. They didn't announce it, they didn't want any press.

"Rosie and Kelli are both low-key about their lesbianism and they didn't want to make a big public show of their wedding," a friend explained.

For the ceremony, Kelli wore a white dress, and the couple exchanged rings and vows they each had written themselves.

At the end of the ceremony, the pair looked into each other's eyes, said "I love you," and kissed, said a source. Then they each hugged their children and vowed to be a family forever.

"After the ceremony, Rosie and Kelli explained to the kids what it all meant," said the friend. "Rosie told them that it meant they were a family and that they all love each other very much. Rosie said that Kelli and she would be there for them no matter what."

Another source said the women considered themselves co-parents of all the children. The kids called Rosie "Mommy," and addressed Kelli by her first name. But plans called for Kelli to also formally adopt each child once Rosie left her show.

"Rosie is completely committed to her kids," the source went on. "They mean more to her than anything. And they are the reason for the wedding. She wanted to show them they were part of a stable, loving family that included Kelli."

"These kids came in and broke the cement around my heart and made a space for Kelli to enter," Rosie added. "And what has grown as a result is an unbelievably beautiful garden."

Wanting more children, Kelli and Rosie quickly tackled the process of conceiving and having their own child together. But first, they had to address the question of who'd be the biological father to fertilize Kelli's egg.

It was a given that Kelli would be the mother. Rosie has said she had little interest in carrying a child herself, and the removal of her fallopian tubes and part of an ovary had made the decision a no-brainer.

But Rosie also may carry a fear of being a biological mother, says psychiatrist Dr. Carole Lieberman.

"Undoubtedly, she is afraid that conceiving a child will physically harm or even kill her, as though the physical act of becoming a mother will kill her like her mother was killed by cancer," Dr. Lieberman said.

But "Rosie has been eager to adopt children and care for them to make up for what she didn't have as a child," noted the renowned psychiatrist. "She wants to create a loving family environment, which she missed out on. And by being a mother to her adopted children, she is trying to make up for the lack of mothering she had."

Kelli and Rosie were united in two decisions on how to make their own baby. First, the process would be artificial insemination with resources from a sperm bank or donor. Second, they would communicate to their obstetrician a description of what sort of male specimen — looks, intelligence, background — they would prefer as biological father. No matter how curious the press or anyone else might be about who the man was, he would not be publicly identified.

The couple considered using a family friend or family member as a sperm donor. They looked at the example of Julie Cypher and rocker Melissa Etheridge, who had turned to rock and roll legend David Crosby to father their two children.

"Tom Cruise was of course number one on the list," a source confided. "David Crosby and Rosie's brother Danny were also talked about."

But Rosie and Kelli decided in the end to use an anonymous donor. They didn't want any legal hassles coming down the road at them, plus they were uncertain of the emotional issues that might be involved in having a friend or family member as the father.

At a New York sperm bank, Rosie and Kelli spent days perusing anonymous profiles to find a suitable donor. "After looking at hundreds of prospective sperm donors, they settled on one who seems to have the right biological stuff," a source confided.

"He looks a lot like the men in both their families."

The father of Rosie and Kelli's baby had the northern European ancestry that Rosie and Kelli shared. According to a source, the donor they chose was a middle-aged, college-educated professional with blond hair and blue eyes — as did Kelli. Plus, he stood 6 feet tall and weighed 170 pounds, with an athletic build and a high IQ. Most important to Rosie, the anonymous donor had no health problems in his family.

"That was Rosie's big concern," the source revealed. "She had a thorough medical history report done to make sure the donor had no genetic predisposition to cancer or heart disease or alcoholism or any other major illnesses."

"Cancer runs in Rosie's family," the source explained. "She lives in fear she'll die of it. She didn't want her children living in fear of disease as she does. There is also alcoholism in Rosie's family and she wanted to make sure the donor had no substance dependency problems."

The doctor explained the realities of the process.

They were told not to expect immediate success. Several efforts to achieve artificial insemination were usually required before a pregnancy was achieved. That didn't faze Rosie and Kelli a bit.

Again careful timing could be helpful. They'd welcome this baby any month of the year, of course. Still, it might bother the syndication company and advertisers less if the next O'Donnell arrived after the show's last taping. There is no sign that Rosie considered that, for she and Kelli went ahead without any delay.

Their baby was what mattered most.

Kelli was impregnated by artificial insemination in March 2002 at a New York fertility clinic. Despite the doctor's warnings about possibly needing several tries or more, Kelli conceived on the first attempt.

Rosie and Kelli were "thrilled," of course — but news of Kelli's pregnancy didn't travel without controversy. There were several family experts who were not nearly thrilled at the prospect of Rosie's child being born into a two-woman household as the parents were.

"Children need both a father and a mother for good emotional health and development," said Glenn T. Stanton, an expert at the family-support group Focus on the Family.

Rev. Louis P. Sheldon of the Traditional Values Coalition also blasted Rosie for her decision to bring a child into a lesbian relationship. "Most lesbian couples do not stay together," Rev. Sheldon added in. "Look at what happened to Anne Heche and Ellen DeGeneres. Melissa Etheridge and Julie Cypher also broke up."

In reality, the decision to conceive a child had not been taken lightly by Rosie and Kelli. And as she crept closer and closer to jumping out of the closet she'd lived in for almost her entire adult life, Rosie was casting the concerns of conservative Middle America to the winds. She was on the cusp of telling the world to love her as she was or leave her.

Meanwhile, Rosie and Kelli wouldn't give up their connection with Mia. The little girl had been placed in the adoptive home Rosie and Kelli had found for her, and they visited regularly. And Rosie was speaking up for change in the Florida adoption law. Since she was a celebrity, her stand was widely reported in the media across the country.

Individuals and groups who were troubled, if not shocked, by what she was urging responded swiftly and sharply. The backlash built week by week as the time for Floridians to vote on keeping or changing the law drew nearer.

People who paid attention to who O'Donnell had

as guests on her show and what she'd said on camera had seen signs of the host's sexuality well before this. Show business types and other insiders had recognized the clear, if not loud, meanings of a dozen brief episodes. Hiding her feelings wasn't what Rosie O'Donnell ever did best.

Those in the entertainment world had nodded knowingly when gay comedienne Ellen DeGeneres "goofed" on Rosie's show about being a "Lebanese." She very obviously isn't, and thousands of people in Hollywood and on Broadway realized she was hinting about being a lesbian. When Rosie replied that she might be "Lebanese" too, insiders got the joke.

Nobody in the entertainment community or anywhere else saw any joke in Rosie's treatment of Anne Heche, however. Heche and DeGeneres had been lovers for years. Everyone knew that, and when that relationship ended, the news of the break was equally widespread. Like anyone abandoned by a lover, DeGeneres was hurt.

That wasn't the end of it.

There was a ripple effect. A lot of gay men and women who had celebrated the "coming out" of DeGeneres as a lesbian were deeply offended by what they viewed as Heche's betrayal. Later, insiders reported, some of these individuals were among those who had been urging Rosie for years to come out as her friend DeGeneres had.

On Sept. 6, 2001, Rosie had verbally beaten up Heche on the show. She wasn't there, but that didn't seem important to Rosie. Heche had done an interview on "20/20" to plug her new and definitely unusual memoir, "Call Me Crazy." There was nothing extraordinary about someone going on a TV interview to publicize a book, film, record, or other commercial enterprise.

In her book, Heche reported a strange personal saga of years in which she wasn't entirely sane, a long time in which she really believed that she spoke to God in a secret language and also had a second personality. Barbara Walters has been fascinated to hear about that one, a space alien named Celestia.

Rosie wasn't fascinated when she talked about that interview on her own show. Many people have speculated that Rosie was still angry about Heche's leaving DeGeneres, a longtime friend. That's never been confirmed, but Rosie couldn't help sneering at what Heche had said and written. While Rosie ended her abusive comments with good wishes to Heche and her husband, it couldn't be denied that she'd derided someone whom the gay community despised as a traitor.

Now in early 2002, Rosie could see the light at the end of the tunnel she'd soon exit. Though the daily talk show had been more than good to her and made her a very rich and famous star, six years were enough. She wasn't ungrateful, but she was ready for the inner Rosie O'Donnell to step out and speak up candidly.

With less than two months more of live telecasts scheduled, she began to talk publicly and clearly about her love life. For years she had been represented and advised by one of the most influential, feared, and brilliant executives in the U.S. public relations business, Lois Smith of the PMK group. A very smart PMK veteran named Cindi Berger also worked closely with Rosie.

They had put out many news reports and colorful accounts about their dynamic client. Among the stories that showed in print were several that "explained" that Rosie didn't need a man in her life because her relationship with her children occupied and fulfilled her. "Protecting" her image was the public relations team's duty.

Rosie's public image was shifting quickly in the winter and spring of 2002. While a growing number of people understood what her crusade for the law change in Florida meant, now she was specifically identifying herself as a gay woman. Appearing at a fund-raiser at Caroline's comedy club in Manhattan, Rosie told it like she saw it and lived it.

That March, Rosie she said being gay was "no big thing" while speaking sharply against one special group that had criticized her. The story that spread rapidly was that she'd brushed aside allegations — charges from "righteous" women — that she'd been dishonest in pretending to be heterosexual.

Rosie dealt with this charge with good humor, it appears. As for the wrath that followed her ongoing compliments about Tom Cruise, the middle O'Donnell child pointed out that she'd never declared she wanted to have sex with him. She told the nightclub audience that all she said she wanted was for Cruise to mow her lawn and bring her a lemonade.

Most of the media missed this story. That wasn't the case when Rosie officially identified herself as a lesbian in a carefully planned television interview on

ABC with Diane Sawyer. It has been reported that Rosie, who's spoken frankly about being in therapy for a long time, had been advised to do this by her therapist.

Rosie had repeatedly mentioned how much stress she endured, and referred to the ongoing need for medication to cope. Concealing a person's sexuality could certainly produce emotional stress, psychologists have said, thus producing a need for tranquilizers.

She was "out" from coast to coast on March 14, 2002.

By then the news seemed less important to the public than other reports from the Rosie front. Kelli Carpenter was pregnant. Father: unidentified. Birth: due in December. Sex of infant: not known yet.

Reporters covering television and Rosie's loyal fans absorbed the "outing" and the pregnancy, and were now much more focused on the imminent end of Rosie's unique and enormously popular talk show.

No one wanted her to quit.

After six years, a mini-era was coming to a close.

Rosie, however, was ready to move on. Years earlier she'd signed a contract for a $3 million advance to write an autobiography. She'd put it off because she didn't think she could cover her sexuality, an important part of anyone's life. Now she didn't have to wait any longer to write her book.

She'd already delivered a very moving manuscript to Warner Books. Unconventional and compelling, the saga titled "Find Me" was moving through the production process. It was to be totally different form her earlier book on how to detect breast cancer, the well-received "Bosom Bodies" she'd co-written with author Deborah Axelrod. "Find Me" was about Rosie, her family, her weaknesses and her fears.

While it didn't dwell on Rosie's love life, as the autobiographies of many stars do, her sexual identity wasn't masked anymore.

"Find Me," so full of pain and self-revelation, was due to go on sale just after Rosie's final "live" telecast. That memorable moment in talk-show history was set. The immensely dynamic, talented, and popular woman who was both the Queen of Nice and the unpredictable reigning sovereign of daytime talk was abdicating.

A number of shows that she'd taped but not broadcast were to be aired nationally over the following few months. The somewhat optimistic and a bit desperate syndicators were trying to shape a new show with another charismatic hostess to hold onto the time slots at the various stations. All this was known as Rosie O'Donnell stepped in front of the cameras for her extravaganza and live finale on May 22nd, 2002.

The big-boned funnylady went out big, of course.

The star didn't do anything small. She was in a state of exuberant exhilaration the day she wrapped up the series that made her so rich, famous and widely admired. Her future looked glorious. She had three healthy children. The woman she loved had gotten pregnant on the first attempt at artificial insemination. A fourth O'Donnell child was due in December.

Rosie had earned six prestigious Emmy Awards from her peers, and something like $120 million from her syndicator partners. Endorsements and commercials, a Rosie-Barbie doll, and other ventures had provided a lot of additional income to fund all the help-the-children causes that meant so much to her.

Her very personal book would be out soon, and she was also looking forward to devoting more time to the year-old magazine.

She was in great spirits as she stepped in front of the studio audience for the final celebration of "The Rosie O'Donnell Show" — live. A mob of talented performers joined in the happy event — Madonna, who danced merrily with Rosie and a gang of dancers from musicals currently on the New York stage, and even her beloved Barbra Streisand in a taped hurrah whooped it up for the glowing president of the class of 1980 at Commack High.

John Lithgow, who came to the Big Apple to star in a musical treatment of "What Makes Sammy Run," gave Rosie a lifetime pass to any and all shows on Broadway. A bare-chested male of the hunk school presented her with a bottle of top-quality French champagne.

The finale was a stunning stroke of genius that dazzled everyone.

There he was — Tom Cruise.

"Rosie, I've mowed your lawn, and now I've brought you your lemonade," he said, delivering the glass. It was funny, emotional and joyous as Rosie waved farewell to her faithful audience. She was standing in front of a spread of theater posters, a fitting end for a warmhearted and generous entertainer who'd done so much to support Broadway.

She was pleased that most of the staff she'd worked with would be going on to a talk show designed as a successor to her six-year triumph. Her friends and fans, insiders and total strangers, were hopeful that all would go well for her now.

They might have known better.

CHAPTER 17

AFTER THE QUEEN OF NICE VANISHED BEHIND THE CURTAINS OF HER SET ON MAY 22, THE ROSIE O'DONNELL THE PUBLIC SAW NEXT WOULD BE A SNEERING, SWAGGERING BUTCH CUTTING DOWN PROMINENT PEOPLE WITH A VICIOUS WIT.

Maybe she was onto something a few years earlier, when she'd said she thought aliens visiting Earth had put an implant in her. She did a stand-up act at the thriving Mohegan Sun Casino in Uncasville, Conn. There hadn't been any talk of her returning to personal appearances, but Tommy Mottola, music mogul high on the Sony empire food chain, had the idea she'd draw a lot of her faithful fans.

Rosie, whose fortune is said to hover around $120 million, was feeling glad to be free of the daily show and in a frisky good mood. She told friends that she wanted to be paid "a million dollars" for the show. That would be close to a Streisand-sized fee, and Rosie would appreciate that. Mottola wasn't daunted. Rosie came to the Indian-owned gambling casino — and she did her number.

"When you have a show, you have to be nice to people," Rosie announced to the crowd. "Now I can say what I want. The bitch ain't so nice anymore."

The quote was all over the press the next day.

There was nobody to inhibit Rosie. She was free of the suits running the syndication company — and of concern about what television station managers, advertising agency vice presidents, corporations paying for commercials to sell their products, or her legion of fans out there with old traditional attitudes might think.

A million dollars to walk out on stage and just say what she thought or felt about anyone and anything — after all these years the very rich but still angry motherless child could tell it exactly as she saw it.

She called herself a "big-mouthed, fat lesbian" before she turned her verbal machine gun on a wide range of prominent men and women who offended her. Her rant was as far from politically correct as anyone could get and she seemed to enjoy every second of it.

One of her targets was President Clinton, who she said had spoken to her the previous night. Rosie was livid about the president's behavior in regard to Monica Lewinsky. "I didn't want to talk to him," Rosie seethed, "because he lied to me when he said 'I did not have sex with that woman.' You put the scarlet letter on her for the rest of her life!"

"He disgusts me!" Rosie screamed, before moving on to other targets. Oprah Winfrey, who hadn't come in from Chicago for the party at the end of O'Donnell's final live broadcast, got off relatively lightly.

"She was busy," Rosie jeered. "She was home counting her money."

It sounded strange coming from the mouth of a star known to be a multi-millionairess, but stranger salvos were to follow.

Anne Heche caught it for having "never really been a lesbian at all."

Building up a head of steam, Rosie seared the globally publicized recent wedding of Liza Minnelli and dapper, effeminate producer David Gest, describing the lavish, star-studded gala as "the gayest thing since my last show." After a few shots at others in the performing community, she delivered her heaviest bombardment to a notoriously conspicuous and easy target.

Taking on Michael Jackson, she said all the things that lawyers would advise anyone not to say. Rosie was merciless, perhaps because she was aware that "Jacko" isn't an active litigator. He stays out of court though he frequently courts attention with his bizarre behavior.

"He's a freak," Rosie pronounced. "He's cream-colored and he has no nasal passages whatsoever. He doesn't look human. Did he look into the mirror one day and say, 'perfect'?" Then she added that she had no contact with Jackson, because "I make it a rule not to speak to pedophiles. Come on. I think you all know that kid was probably telling the truth or else Michael wouldn't have paid him off."

The casino audience recognized her reference to 1993 charges that Jackson had molested a 13-year-old boy, a case that was dropped amid reports the child's parents had been given $20 million to settle.

O'Donnell was apparently among those unimpressed by the fact that no evidence of child molestation had been presented in any trial.

While this barrage at the casino was a shocker, there had been a hint that something confrontational might be coming from the Queen of Nice. Some weeks earlier, Rosie had welcomed an invitation to appear on Fox TV's "The O'Reilly Factor." O'Reilly had earned a national reputation as a bulldog conservative, and Rosie could not resist a chance to debate revision of the Florida adoption law.

It was a spirited but respectful collision between brainy advocates of opposite positions. It was also something more. The conversation expanded to other matters on Rosie's mind. High on her agenda was Bill and Hillary Clinton, a concern rooted in the Lewinsky scandal. O'Donnell had been known as a liberal Democrat who had supported Mrs. Clinton's successful campaign for U.S. Senate.

That ended before the telecast did.

"I assumed that as soon as she was elected senator she would divorce," Rosie told O'Reilly bluntly. "I'm shocked that she did not."

When the right-wing interviewer replied that this showed that Mrs. Clinton's "lust for power" overcame her dignity, Rosie immediately agreed. She added that she herself was still "terrifically" offended by the ex-president's actions with the intern.

While there were no public statements by either the former first lady or the former Queen of Nice, word leaked out that Mrs. Clinton was so hurt by Rosie's comments that she wouldn't even "take" the phone call Rosie made to explain and heal. A number of other women had also speculated that Mrs. Clinton ought to dump her straying spouse when she went to work as a senator, but they were strangers, while Rosie was somebody she knew and trusted.

There was more trouble brewing for Rosie as political and religious leaders encouraged Floridians to oppose changing the adoption law when voting day arrived. Bruised by the rift with Mrs. Clinton, Rosie now turned her attention from supporting a general Democratic agenda to Kelli's advancing pregnancy — something much more immediate and personal.

Rosie had finished a tour around Florida to press for the revision of the statute, and she hoped she'd persuaded some people. She could do more than hope in regard to the baby Kelli was carrying. She could take care of Kelli, as Kelli had taken care of her when she had cut the tendons in her hand.

But something else was coming to a head.

It, too, was more important than relations with the Clintons or the various liberal causes she'd been backing over the years. Since she had more time to devote to the magazine now that she had shed the talk show, the energetic star was taking a greater interest in every aspect of the monthly that bore her name.

From the first issue of "Rosie" in the spring of 2001, Rosie O'Donnell hadn't been exactly the kind of partner and editorial director whom the magazine professionals recruited by Gruner & Jahr expected. One of the things that surprised them was her attitude about who should be on the periodical's cover. Oprah lit up the front page of her magazine frequently, and that sold copies, especially at newsstands. Publishing smarties figured Rosie's face could do that too.

It never occurred to any of the with-it young women that she'd reject the idea. After all, Rosie was a megastar who'd never shown any signs of shyness. She was accustomed to the spotlight, and they figured all stars had egos the size of skyscrapers.

Everyone accepted the "fact," except Rosie.

No way would her face be on all the covers, she said. She'd had enough publicity in connection with the talk show. This was the print world, more dignified than the circus of popular entertainment and show business. Television was all about celebrities hamming it up while pushing sales of movies or records or sometimes a TV special.

That was all fine and profitable for everyone involved, but Rosie seemed ready to take a more serious approach to her magazine. To make that clear, she told the editors that it should be the contents of the magazine that were emphasized, so she didn't need her photo on the cover. While she meant to have ongoing input as the editorial director, she wanted covers that dealt with the articles inside.

The editors didn't go for it.

Like the Gruner & Jahr executives who'd poured tens of millions of dollars into the effort to try to save something out of the sagging circulation and advertising revenues of "old" "McCall's," they believed that Rosie's name and face were needed to make the new monthly a success.

"The Rosie O'Donnell Show" was still on the air

five days a week when the "Rosie" magazine was
launched. The corporate backers gave it plenty of
promotion but also assumed that the lively star's
activities before the camera would be a major
additional push. By the time the first issue was on
sale, Rosie needed all the promotion it could get,
because circulation was down under 700,000.

The big-boned star did mention items in the
magazine on camera from time to time, but she
didn't become a pitchwoman for the publication. She
focused, instead, on pushing an agenda that didn't
feature the standard fare of women's magazines
— the beautiful people. She was convinced that a
variety of women and men deserved the magazine's
recognition in articles and on the cover. The
publishing veterans kept pointing out that the
experience in this business was that glamorous
celebrities on the cover moved the most copies.

Those executives were not very happy with Rosie's
odd preference to keep herself off the cover but
instead give that exposure to such people as
wheelchair-bound Christopher Reeves or talented
soul singer Macy Gray. The editors had tried to spell
out politely their views of the realities of publishing
a women's magazine, but Rosie didn't appear to
recognize that this was a publication trying to appeal
to a large number of fairly conventional women.

And she wasn't a conventional, middle-of-the-road
woman.

Her approach was interpreted by the editors as
unreceptive to standard, time-honored, and safe
ways of reaching out to American women. They were
correct. That was only part of the problem. Long a

star who had more power than patience, Rosie didn't understand why they couldn't see that they were behind the times.

Not only was she imaginative and creative, but Rosie had a contract that said she was editorial director. As half owner and editorial director, she was ready to direct a magazine that reflected — not ignored — her own views and interests. She'd managed to put up with and work in cooperation with the take-no-chances policies of the corporate men at the Warner syndication enterprise. She saw no reason to play that game anymore.

Her magazine — that's what it was, because it bore her name — would be forward-looking. It would sail past the old attitudes of the existent herd of women's monthlies stuck in the rut of fashion and gossip. It would stand out as fresh, different, and compassionate toward many people the other women's publications were ignoring.

As an overweight and outspoken individual who didn't look, dress, or like the great majority, Rosie wasn't put off by the idea of a cover offering a crippled man in a wheelchair. Maybe it wasn't exactly glamorous, but it was honest and it asked readers to face human diversity.

Whether she was urging all those conventional women to accept the unconventional or just advocating a compassionate human-interest article about extraordinary courage, Rosie did not win over the magazine professionals on this one. She had more success in her determined effort to get Macy Gray, who hadn't yet become a big star, on the cover. With Rosie's circulation flagging, the Gruner & Jahr executive overseeing the magazine decided to replace editor Cathy Cavender, a favorite of Rosie O'Donnell, with Susan Toepfer, another experienced magazine editor who'd earned a get-it-done reputation at "People." Gruner & Jahr was already uneasy about reports that O'Donnell was pressing the staff very hard to get her way. This new editor would be strong enough to solve that. But Rosie was immediately unhappy with the choice of Toepfer and with the firing of Cavender. Gruner & Jahr says that Rosie unsuccessfully tried to have Toepfer fired — and that she threatened to "sabotage" the magazine unless it capitulated to Rosie's "increasingly intemperate demands."

Now Toepfer met with increasing pressure from Rosie to get the Macy Gray cover. The new editor reluctantly yielded, so the January 2002 issue had the African-American soul singer on the front page. Rosie was confident that the editors were underestimating the savvy of the public and that readers would buy this number eagerly.

Rosie was wrong.

Sales dropped by more than half at newsstands. After investing hundreds of hours in interviews with the star and assorted editors involved in the issue, veteran Rosie-watcher Judith Newman reported to "Vanity Fair" readers that O'Donnell was "practically apoplectic" when somebody was bold enough to suggest that "an eccentric such as Macy Gray" might not sell as many copies as pretty Jennifer Aniston of Friends fame would.

It had been more than five years since anyone had told Rosie she was wrong. She reacted as many rich and famous people would. She went ballistic, Newman heard.

Rosie hailed Gray as "one of the great artists of our generation" to editors whose jobs depended less on artistry than on covers that sold magazines. They listened sensibly and silently as Rosie shouted.

"Little did I know that you're not allowed to put black women on the cover!" she accused.

One editor commented: "Rosie would see social injustice where it doesn't exist." It is a fact, however, that African-American females have appeared on a very small percentage of the covers of U.S. women's magazines.

Covers weren't the only problem the well-meaning Rosie had on her hands at her magazine. As a celebrity, she'd learned that media interviews with celebrities drew audiences. Not being a magazine professional, she didn't fully understand or totally accept the ground rules and ethics involved in doing interviews properly.

Or was it that she so deeply wanted the other rich and famous to like her?

Could it have been she hoped that keeping them happy would get her future celebrity interviews?

Whatever she had in mind, she insisted on doing something that bothered her staff and their journalism school proprieties. When she did the interview with the then revered and now also controversial Martha Stewart, Rosie asked the astoundingly wealthy tycoon what sort of car she drove.

"A Suburban," the one-woman conglomerate replied honestly.

There would have been no issue of journalistic

ethics if friendly Rosie hadn't sent Steward a draft of the article before it was to go to the printer and Stewart hadn't coolly changed the answer to "Chrysler."

She had a reason. Millions of them, in fact.

Chrysler and the Stewart empire had just signed a contract that combined a sweepstakes, radio and television promotion, and millions of dollars of advertising in Stewart's own magazine, which was thriving but would never turn away more revenue.

One of Stewart's crew assured Rosie that Stewart also had a Chrysler at the time of the interview, so the corrected reply ran.

There were other things that O'Donnell, who was inexperienced in the proprieties of journalism, did that troubled the staff. From time to time, she acted as if the magazine was her personal plaything.

Using the magazine to benefit her friends and relatives, the editors complained — to each other, that is; they didn't dare tell her this. Kelli's grandma was the subject of an admiring column, though editors saw her as "a sweet old lady with nothing to say." Rosie also ordered an article on the wedding of editor-at-large Heidi Safer, who just happened to be Kelli's stepsister.

Safer functioned as Rosie's in-house representative when Rosie was away. She was the protector and "interpreter of Rosie's vision." Though Rosie had a properly large editorial director's office in the plush suite at 375 Lexington Avenue in Midtown-Manhattan, she wasn't expected to be there every day.

She was in frequent contact with the top editors,

sounding off freely and imaginatively in the creative spirit that made her Rosie. She phoned in, e-mailed, and came and went as she pleased. When the talk show ended, it meant she could leave New York whenever she wanted for as long as she wished.

In one such trip, when Rosie heard about a provocative new musical comedy on stage in London, she packed her platinum credit card and jetted across the Atlantic to check it out. She saw the show, loved it and decided she'd do a U.S. production.

The show was "Tattoo," based on the life of a very talented British "performance artist" who wasn't exactly heterosexual but was definitely extraordinary. One of the stars of this enormously popular hit on London's famed West End was witty, talented, musical, and sophisticated Boy George, who'd been a gender-bending, dashing, mascara-laden pop singer in the 1980s with a British group called Culture Club.

Rosie went backstage after the performance, full of enthusiasm to meet the very hip and even more chic Boy George. A passionate admirer of musical theater, like her late mother, Rosie got right to the point.

It's not clear whether Boy George fully appreciated who and how big a star Rosie was, or whether he was just being cooler than cool — standard Boy George. In either case, he wasn't interested in having her produce "Tattoo" on Broadway.

"You're too suburban," he told the American woman, who was anything but.

Instead of arguing with him or unleashing a furious temper, Rosie flew back to New York to plan her next move.

She didn't even consider giving up her idea.

Rosie had the money and the dream, so there was no way she'd be denied. If Boy George had the power to grant her what she wanted, and if he didn't think she looked sophisticated enough to produce "Tattoo" with the right vision, she'd change his mind.

First she would change her hairstyle. The idea that changing your hair would help you get what you want probably wouldn't occur to people less intuitive and savvy than Rosie, but perhaps that was why she was Rosie the star. Rolling the dice, she went to one of New York's top hair wizards and showed him a photo of a cool and fearless-looking rock "chick" who'd sung with Culture Club back when Boy George worked with them.

"I want that cut," Rosie demanded.

No sensible person would have done it, but Rosie was confident that offbeat Boy George was more cool than sensible, and she returned to London. Boy, was she right.

Boy George eyed the haircut, recognized the message, and accepted her offer. Back in New York, Rosie started to make plans.

But first was the big excitement of her and Kelli's baby, their fourth child, who was due to arrive soon in December 2002. Kelli was healthy, and the situation looked under control. Everything was normal with Blake, Chelsea and Parker, the three adopted children Rosie loved so deeply.

She touched base at the magazine, as a co-owner and editorial director should, a routine step to reassure the staff and herself. Even though Heidi was conscientious, intelligent, and vigilant as protector of

Rosie's values, while the star was away, O'Donnell had less than total confidence in the rest of the staff and the editor in chief, who Gruner & Jahr had brought in a few months earlier.

Rosie learned there was another cover crisis at the magazine. It came at the same time there was pressure to improve circulation by moving away from the serious issues Rosie explored and more toward the other mainstream magazines for women. Editor Toepfer wanted to get away from the "dark" content to make it a happy home for fashion and beauty stories — and the ads those would bring.

Rosie had been so indifferent to those goals that when she had posed for some of the cover photos, she had done so reluctantly and without makeup. She hadn't said so, but she meant to signal that plain, plump, or otherwise unglamorous women were just as worthy as glamorous beauties. Rosie had no illusions about her own appearance. She wasn't about to compete with skinny starlets.

That may have sparked the explosion.

Back in the office, the new editor presented Rosie with a design for the cover of an issue that included a trendy article about the women in "The Sopranos" television series. Rosie was already steaming from reading another magazine article headlined "Rosie Hits 300 Pounds," but now she boiled over. The cover mock-up showed Rosie between trim and sexy Edie Falco and Lorraine Bracco, popular and attractive actresses each more than 50 pounds lighter than the furious co-owner of her own magazine.

The article about Rosie's weight in the other magazine was one of several that various magazines were running. In addition, there'd been some tasteless jokes on television by entertainers whom Rosie still despised. Still, when she saw how big she looked on the proposed cover, she lost it.

She had been sensible enough never to use them on any TV broadcast, but Rosie had acquired as many four-letter words as most of the other entertainers of her generation. She let them fly at the editor about the cover design, swearing she didn't want to see her "fat %&*$# stomach on the cover of this magazine."

Rosie got her way. An immediate redesign removed O'Donnell from the picture, and "The Sopranos'" Aida Turturro was Photoshopped in.

The air in the office remained tense. O'Donnell flatly refused to appear on any future covers of her magazine, but she posed for the cover of "People." Somehow, she was beautifully made up and styled.

There was more conflict ahead. O'Donnell wrote in a piece for her regular Editor's Letter that the previous editor in chief would be coming back. That was never published, and the previous editor, who Rosie had liked better, did not return.

To assert who was in control, Dan Brewster of Gruner & Jahr called a meeting at which he reminded the staff that O'Donnell's contract stipulated that her editorial control was subject to veto by Gruner & Jahr's chief executive officer. As that CEO, he laid down the law. She was away at the time, but when Rosie returned, she was outraged.

She attended several subsequent staff meetings, asserting her authority and threatening to close the publication if hostile and embarrassing leaks to the press didn't halt immediately. In fact, reports of a hostile, berating, downright nasty Rosie emerged from those meetings with staffers of the magazine.

Rosie was alleged to have "Exorcist qualities" by employees who said they had suffered her outbursts in meetings. She was said to have told one woman, a breast-cancer survivor, "You know what happens to people when they lie, don't you? They get cancer!"

"She had this way of screaming, 'Did you not hear me? Well you better do that!'" one unnamed staffer confided. "It was like a kid being abused — like a parent trying to tell them why they're being slapped around for their own good."

A new picture was emerging of the woman who over the years had told everybody all about how her mother had died of cancer and that she had suffered an abusive childhood. The Queen of Nice was dead — and Rosie didn't care.

"If anybody believes that the show was the totality of who I was . . . they're crazy," Rosie said in answer to her critics. "It was an afternoon show, and I did what was a venue-appropriate show. This is not the defining essence of me."

She said in another interview that her show "required one thing: It was a specific kind of canvas. It was afternoon TV. It was Merv Griffin or Mike Douglas. It was non-controversial. It was happy, fun, light, mothers-at-home, and 'Relate to them, Rosie, in the best way you can.'"

Few were finding it easy to relate to Rosie anymore — least of all her "partners" at Rosie.

Things at the magazine, in fact, descended

into open warfare between the star and the "suit,"
Brewster, who saw a threat to his firm's huge
investment which far exceeded the $6 million Rosie
had put in. He wasn't about to yield.

Neither was Rosie.

Circulation was down to 300,000. Determined
not to let them turn the magazine that bore her name
and identity into something she'd loathe, O'Donnell
consulted a high-powered female lawyer. Petite Mary
Jo White had earned a big reputation as a very
effective attorney in New York. For their part, Rosie's
deep-pocketed corporate partner signed up a former
assistant secretary of the interior as their legal spear
carrier.

The staff shivered and waited. Rosie had seen
therapists over the years, and now it was the
editors' turn to do that. G & J and O'Donnell each
had big cash, but the threat that the magazine
would close and leave them jobless scared the
editors. Some 70 employees worried about next
month's paychecks as threats and offers flew back
and forth.

What was said depends on who you believe.
O'Donnell has claimed that Brewster offered to sell
the name and magazine "Rosie" back to her for $20
million. For the record, Gruner & Jahr lost much
more than that on the magazine since its transition
away from "McCall's" began. Rosie insisted that this
was the U.S.A., and American laws said she still
owned her name, so there was no reason for her to
pay these people a dollar.

A dollar? In fact, that was the figure Brewster
quoted. He told people that the corporation had

offered to sell the magazine and its complete subscription list to Rosie for a dollar.

On Sept. 18th, Rosie O'Donnell called her own meeting of the staff to announce that she was ending this intolerable situation by closing the magazine. The December 2002 issue would be the last.

Aware that this would be a blow to the working people who lived on Rosie paychecks, she made it clear that she didn't want to hurt them even if she couldn't stand Gruner & Jahr. Out of her own pocket, Rosie gave to each of 30 staff members a check for $10,000, personally handed out in the office by Kelli's sister Heidi Safer. Notably, the group who received checks did not include the editor in chief, with whom Rosie had never been compatible.

In the days that followed, there was speculation that Brewster might have deliberately and cleverly pushed Rosie's buttons to get her so angry that she'd stop the magazine. That would relieve his employer of the legal and fiscal responsibility for the multimillion-dollar disaster.

The immediate consequences of the announcement were bitter and predictable. Gruner & Jahr marketing officer Cathy Sponger issued a scorching statement that Rosie "has walked away from her television show, her brand, her public personality, her civility — and now her fans, the advertising community, her business partner and her contractual responsibilities."

Rosie responded by taking the battle to her own turf. She struck back on half a dozen TV talk shows, where she was warmly welcomed as an established star with armies of loyal fans.

She seemed resolute and energetic, not a bit afraid

of any huge conglomerate, as she defended what she "had to do" and criticized Gruner & Jahr.

The media found all this conflict fascinating, and press people were equally impressed by the next development. First Gruner & Jahr sued her for a headline-making $300 million, which sought triple damages and which, the firm said, would cover its losses in the magazine. In the same spirit of righteous acrimony, O'Donnell countersued Gruner & Jahr for $125 million. She claimed that editorial control of Rosie had been unfairly wrested from her — and she said she would not let someone put her good name on a product she no longer believed in.

Where the Gruner & Jahr lawsuit included a litany of details of Rosie's alleged abuse toward staffers and her unwillingness to be realistic about what was needed to sell the magazine, Rosie's interview blitz was aimed at explaining her side of the story and repair the immense damage done to her image by the brouhaha.

"Contract or no contract, my name was on the magazine and it had to reflect my vision," Rosie explained.

She pointed to an example of what she'd been up against at the magazine:

"I was going to do an interview with Carol Burnett, who had a play running that she'd written with her daughter Carrie Hamilton. Carrie died of cancer in January as the play was opening. I didn't want to push Carol about the death. But editor Susan Toepfer told me, 'You can't just talk about the play!'

"I told her: 'The death is a terrible tragedy. I don't want to push her on that.' Toepfer leaned forward and said, 'You mean you are going to ignore the dead kid?' I was so shocked, all I could say was, 'Oh, my God.'"

In the midst of all the turmoil related to the magazine and the lawsuits flying back and forth, Rosie and Kelli suffered a scare related to Kelli's pregnancy.

Kelli had been suffering from stomachaches, spotting and migraine headaches. And the emotional fray over the magazine only made the symptoms worse.

One day during the fracas with Gruner & Jahr, Kelli's stomach began to feel like the tightening spasms of labor contractions, a source said.

"Kelli told Rosie to call the doctor, who told them to get to the hospital immediately," the source explained. "Kelli and Rosie were absolutely beside themselves with panic. They prayed on the way."

Luckily, when they got to the hospital, Kelli's spasms were diagnosed as Braxton-Hicks contractions, or false labor. Their precious baby-to-be was in great shape — although Kelli continued to suffer a blinding headache.

"Rosie and Kelli are extremely nervous about the pregnancy, and the stress they are under because of the lawsuit makes everything worse," the source said.

"They have planned the rest of their lives around the fact that they are rich and can pursue parenthood without any money issues. That's why Rosie did her talk show for so long — so she'd be independently wealthy for the rest of her life. Now, if they lose the lawsuit — a very real possibility — Rosie and Kelli will be wiped out. That's difficult to face, and that's why they feel so much stress."

Fingers crossed for the baby, and for their financial future, Rosie and Kelli were forced to take things one day at a time.

CHAPTER 18

IN LATE FALL 2002, ROSIE O'DONNELL WAS STILL TRYING TO HELP OTHER PEOPLE. SHE'D DONE THAT FOR SO MANY YEARS BY GIVING MONEY, MORAL SUPPORT, AND PERSONAL APPEARANCES TO AID A WIDE VARIETY OF CAUSES. HER FIRST EMPHASIS, AS ALWAYS, WAS HER COMMITMENT TO CHILDREN'S ORGANIZATIONS, BUT NOW SHE ADDED TO THAT BY TRYING TO PROMOTE A TELEVISION SERIES IN WHICH SHE HAD NO ECONOMIC INTEREST.

Rosie didn't have the authority to decide who would be the star on the talk show that Warner syndication launched to replace "The Rosie O'Donnell Show." She was aware, however, how big a challenge that would be and that a good number of her former staff were working hopefully on the launch.

Rosie also knew and liked the funny woman who had been chosen to host it, so she figured she might as well do the decent thing and bless the new program with her appearance. To let all her own fans hear that she backed the replacement team, Rosie joined bubbly new host Caroline Rhea on an early broadcast.

She also took Rhea with her to a performance of "Hairspray," which was O'Donnell's favorite show on Broadway. The spirit and music of "Hairspray" were so infectious that it was common for delighted fans to dance in the aisles to the final songs. It might have been unbridled enthusiasm combined with a wish to show her warm affinity with Rhea that made Rosie dance with the younger woman in the aisles — and inform the media they'd celebrated together.

November also brought a disappointment for Rosie. Voters in Florida went to the polls after having considered Rosie's controversial initiative to change the law barring gay adoption. It was soundly defeated. The issue could be raised again, supporters of the call for revision reasoned. It had failed in a year in which conservative candidates and policies showed increased strength, but public attitudes on this issue might shift.

One thing that wasn't changing was Rosie O'Donnell's firm belief that she was right. When the final issue of "Rosie" went to the printer the third week of November, there wasn't a trace of defeat or discouragement in her last column. It was something special.

The woman who was now so much more than a funny lady went out with a poem she'd written. It was serious and moving. It was generous, too, honoring several key people — including the deposed Cathy Cavender — who'd helped her put her voice to the magazine. "Honor the art inside you," the poem read in part. "I am proud of what we all did together."

Vibrant, exuberant Rosie couldn't resist adorning another page of the issue with a slam at the medical experts, television executives, celebrities, and assorted other busy bodies who'd annoyed her for so long with their constant chatter about her weight. She announced that she'd lost eleven pounds but was now giving up the weight-loss "challenge," and quoted a lyric from 'Big, Blonde and Beautiful' in the musical Hairspray: "Sugar, don't be shy," she wrote. "I'm a growing girl."

On Nov. 29th, somebody Rosie was excitedly waiting to meet arrived in New York about 10 days early. That somebody was small but even sweeter than the song. Blonde, 19 inches long, and weighing 6 pounds, 6 ounces, Vivienne Rose O'Donnell was born in a Manhattan hospital. Her parents, Rosie O'Donnell and Kelli Carpenter, were described by a "New York Post" reporter as "ecstatic."

With the demise of "Rosie" and its associated lawsuits, Rosie was in an emotional netherworld at the time of Vivienne Rose's birth. But the arrival of the baby helped Rosie see, again, the things that are really important in life.

Kelli suffered through the 18-hour labor like a trouper, said a source. And Rosie was by her side throughout — just as Kelli had slept on the floor of the ICU when Rosie's hand infection laid her out.

The baby's last name would be O'Donnell. A source explained that the name Vivienne was taken from a character in the book "The Divine Secrets of the Ya-Ya Sisterhood." Rosie nodded to her mother by giving her the middle name Rose.

Rosie finally had a baby to join the three she'd adopted and, of course, loved greatly. Kelli was an enormously proud new mother in her mid-30s, breast-feeding several times a day. Kelli and O'Donnell were happily sharing the diapering and other routines.

For the moment, just about all the talk about how butch Rosie had become in recent months, with her mannish clothes, the Culture Club haircut, and tough talk and foul language, faded into the background. A baby takes priority.

How will this infant affect who Rosie O'Donnell is next year? The person she was in public during her climb to stardom on the talk show was someone different from the hard-edged personality and no-nonsense lesbian who showed up when the syndicated series was done.

That individual is the human being many people have chosen to call "the new Rosie," but O'Donnell insists that's a mistake, too. She says that like any other professional entertainer, she tailored her act, on stage and off, to each audience and situation.

Several fellow entertainers have agreed, pointing to some of her previous nightclub performances that the mainstream press missed completely. At Caesar's Palace in Las Vegas in February 1998 a very rough and definitely ready Rosie belted down a large vodka and capped a barrage of sexy remarks by loosening her pants with a threat to "moon" a ringsider. And she wisecracked that Woody Allen had adopted a young girl so he might bed her when she was sixteen — an apparent jest about Allen and the much younger woman he later married.

While many other stand-ups have done crass acts at various times in their careers, some of the people at Caesar's Palace that evening were startled and some dismayed. They'd expected the wholesome Rosie they knew from her television series, which was watched mostly by housewives. O'Donnell and everyone else involved in daytime shows knew that ultra-adult humor with blue language and lewd gestures would be too much for many homemakers.

So when charges of an ugly "new" Rosie arose, O'Donnell answered she was a comic who'd done adult acts when they seemed right for a location and audience and the other softer material for the very different audience who watched TV in the daytime.

A lot of people have accepted her distinction, but many have not. It isn't just the harsh material that bothers them. Her outspoken lesbian talk makes them think this is a "new" and less kind Rosie. A bitterly funny insult comic isn't the talent they've known.

Yes, she's left the Queen of Nice behind, but she doesn't feel at all guilty. That title was imposed on her by a reporter looking for a clever phrase. "When that came out, I remember saying, 'You know what? Next year it's gonna be the 'Queen of Lice' and the 'The Queen of Fried Rice,'" she joked. "My art form is not based in kindness; it's based in rage."

One way some entertainment professionals look at the Rosie of today versus the one audiences knew is to point to actors and actresses who maintained slim figures for image and income reasons until they were 40 or so. Then they stopped controlling their appetites because they weren't playing skinny parts anymore. They don't have to restrict what they eat, so at 45 they have the money they earned and surprisingly large bellies.

Rosie's friends say this fits her situation. They're not surprised by the butch Rosie because almost everyone in "the business" plus more than a few "civilians" outside have been aware of her sexuality for years.

Even if Rosie wasn't completely honest and there is a "new" O'Donnell, insiders are gossiping about another personality. Is the tough-talking, man's-suit-wearing "new" Rosie here to stay? She's got every right in a free society to any garb that isn't against indecency laws, but might she not change again?

Everyone who has seen Rosie with Vivienne Rose has commented on the extraordinary tenderness that this mother shows. As 2002 turned into 2003, Rosie and her family retreated from public view to care for the baby, and to take a break from the circus atmosphere that had surrounded them for more than half a decade.

But Rosie will be back. The question that remains is whether the world will accept her on her terms, as she really is, as she's always really wanted.

ACKNOWLEDGMENTS

The authors would like to thank Rosie O'Donnell for never being boring, and for opening her heart in numerous interviews over the years. No matter where her life takes her next, she's sure to draw a crowd - and perhaps a Volume II to this biography!

The authors also would like to thank the willing and able reporting staffs at The National Enquirer, Star, and Globe, who have interviewed Rosie O'Donnell and many of her friends and associates through the years. Keep on telling it like it is!

The authors would also like to thank the talented and unflappable researchers at American Media, Inc., for always coming through.